'Whatever g[illegible] have
received, use it in service
to one another.'

1 Peter 4: 10 New English Bible

In obedience to the above instruction
we share in this book, how the Life & Love
of Father God, through Christ, has been,
and is, experienced in the ordinary life
of an ordinary person.

The Great message is:-

All may be touched and changed by
Divine Love.

Worlds Within A World

A Biography

Dorothy Dyson Wood

AuthorHouse™ UK Ltd.
500 Avebury Boulevard
Central Milton Keynes, MK9 2BE
www.authorhouse.co.uk
Phone: 08001974150

First published by AuthorHouse 4/27/2009

ISBN: 978-1-4389-2801-2 (sc)
ISBN: 978-1-4389-2802-9 (hc)

The author can be contacted by email at Jethrodyson@live.co.uk

Printed in the United States of America
Bloomington, Indiana

This book is printed on acid-free paper.

A Greeting From The Author

In this book I pray you'll gain
As we share our joy and pain,
A warming ray from Realms Above
Of hopefulness and touch of Love.
Or maybe just a Shaft of Light
To birth a sweeter Faith insight.

On duller days to see you through!
Let's share a laugh with joke or two.
To see the dafter side of life
Is better than an internal strife!
To lessen, ease, a hidden ache,
To forward go!
The future make!

Contents

Preface

HERE ARE CHAPTERS FROM THE life of Geoffrey Ralph Wood, an ordinary sort of man who has had some extra-ordinary experiences - striking, heart stopping, gut wrenching and overwhelming! And indeed at times, quite hilarious! Compared with the ambitious, his aims in life have been quite modest, his formal education minimal.

But suddenly and unexpectedly, life opened out in a miraculous and joyful way ... after retirement. This remarkable later experience and development was not sought after ... it came to him - it happened

This biography is told by his wife Dorothy who has shared as a participant in some of the special events in her husband's life but empathetically in the more unusual personal experiences, especially in his later life. As this man Geoff, is happier with a screwdriver or wood-saw in his hand than a pen or P.C. word-processor, his wife Dorothy was suddenly inspired to write his biography, prompted by the suggestion from a friend from the past. She met this friend in the latter's home with a relative, on just one occasion, on a trip to the Bradford West Yorkshire village of her birth. There had been a complete break in contact for around fifty years! -Which proves the power of the spoken word even in passing!

Each chapter is complete in itself and each one deals with either a period or aspect of Geoff's life.

It is hoped that the reading of Geoff's story will entertain but also inspire hope and faith and on the way, raise a gasp and a chuckle or two.

Some names have been changed.

All poems are by Dorothy

FAMILY PHOTOS

Percy - Geoff's father plowing with horses Heather & Flower

Gladys Lillian - Geoff's mother aged 55 in 1957

Bill – Geoff's step-father

Geoff aged 9

Geoff 21yrs - 1947 home from Egypt

Geoff aged 21 whilst serving in Egypt

Joyce – Geoff's sister aged 21 in 1942

Dorothy - Geoff's second wife by the narrowboat in 2003

Geoff & Dorothy in 1990

Introduction

GEOFF LOVES WESTERN FILMS - cowboy yarns and war stories. He loves the film "The good, bad, and the ugly" featuring Paul Newman, Robert Redford, and other notable actors.

It struck me that we all experience life's good, bad and ugly! If you add, 'The sad, mad and the hilarious!' to this film title you have a fair mix of the ingredients of life! It also struck me that my husband truly has lived through some extreme samples of this kaleidoscope of human experience. There is in fact, enough of the dramatic and notable to make the recording and passing on of some of these happenings a worthwhile venture.

Here also is the telling of a life that experienced the insecurities of a family split in the early years; later suffered and withstood sudden disintegration in the middle years through the shattering experiences of loss, disillusionment and betrayal. But with faith and optimism, a good and new life was created out of the ashes of the old - like a phoenix rising.

Geoff entered his working life with no formal education beyond the age of ten! and therefore with no qualifications. Perhaps it is inevitable that job-wise he moved around, but he always had confidence that he would find some form of work and could quickly pick up the skills of whatever job he tackled

A reluctant three years spent in the Army, mostly in Egypt just after the war, left him with very strong impressions and memories.

A variety of work situations has given him a wealth of anecdotal material from the colourful chapters of his life A whole book could be written about his experiences as a taxi driver, as a young single man. - Taxiing - a veritable school of life if ever there was one, often in the raw! I include some of these memories here.

The taxi firm Montax was located in the South Wales dock town of Newport. Geoff worked there just after the war. The cars in the fleet were mostly Austin 12s and 14s.

In this job Geoff learned much about the seamy side of life!

Some of his fares were prostitutes coming and going from their customers, frequently they would be merchant seamen who were often the worse for drink. Some had no knowledge of English and there would be a flurry of hand waving and gesturing!

There was a regular customer with the appearance of the actor Charles Laughton; he was a very talented but sadly, alcoholic bachelor barrister of mature years. But one night when he arrived home tumbling out of the taxi practically legless, his irate mother greeted him on the steps of their home and proceeded to punch him all the way down the hall as she admonished him for being 'a naughty boy' for arriving home in a state of inebriation. Sadly this was a regular occurrence. Yet he was much respected for his work. On one occasion he had to be carried bodily into the taxi where soon on the journey he vomited, and revoltingly, Geoff's uniform was also contaminated. The taxi was off the road for an hour's cleaning after this fouling episode; but Geoff extracted £2 from the man's mother for the loss of earnings and inconvenience! However, the solicitor, in his normal drunken stupor after his usual evening of boozing would normally tip generously, too generously in fact!

One late evening one of the other drivers came back to the garage from his shift and told the following story - "You'll never guess what happened this evening! I picked up this couple and they asked to go down to the docks, when I got there they told me to pull up on to a quiet patch of spare ground. Immediately they opened the rear door, (which was hinged on the opposite side to modern cars today) and before I could do or say anything, they lay down on the taxi floor with legs sticking out and immediately they were performing! ...The cheeky b-----s! * # * - So I just strolled away for a few minutes!"

There was the time when Geoff was hauled into an all night party that was short of young men, and the hosts paid for the time in the night hours that was ticking away on the taxi clock! Flaunting company rules, there were times when girl friends were taken along for a trip ... and there were other misdemeanours! But all that is another story!

People aim for significance and self satisfaction by various commonly accepted goals and means: - by progressing in their sphere of work or study, by becoming famous, by family life in the rearing of children, by travel, for some, by the amassing of wealth, and so on. But none of these commonly accepted roads to self-fulfilment apply to this man. He simply took up new opportunities as they arose.

Life can be bad, very bad, but we must not give up on life when pain heaps upon pain because something wonderful and glorious may be just around the corner or waiting in the future, just for me...just for you!

Well, the something - 'very special' happened to Geoff my husband, after his official working life was over.

Author,
Geoffrey's wife, Dorothy

CHAPTER ONE

EARLY DAYS ON THE FARM

GEOFFREY RALPH WOOD

GEOFF WAS BORN IN 1926 - between the two World Wars in deep countryside in Hatfield, Hertfordshire. He was the second son and the fourth and youngest child of a quiet farmer, Percy, and his wife, Gladys Lillian. She chose to be known as Lill. She was born and raised in N. Clapham London, within the sound of Bow Bells. She was nicknamed 'Townie'. A Cockney, she was fun loving and enjoyed company. The man she married was very much a quiet countryman. Percy about 5' 5", was slight but tough.

Percy worked mostly with horses for what was known as a gentleman farmer. The farm was huge and did everything! All the farm animals you can think of were reared on this farm! There were harvests of all kinds, vegetable, fruit and grain. An amazing number of farm hands were employed, all with their various skills.

The family lived in a hamlet named Roegreen (now fully built-up) with a pub 'The Old Fiddle' village shop, duck pond and scattered cottages.

The family lived in No 2 of a block of 4 cottages with rough textured grey rendering on the front walls. A tar-gravelled lane ran in front and a compacted earth access lane ran behind the cottages leading to woodland and open fields. Roegreen was 0.25miles from the A1 (now the A1M) London was 20miles away.

The cottages had small front gardens, mostly growing flowers. The rear gardens mostly grew produce but across the gravel lane in front were allotments. At No1 lived a cowman, at No3 another horseman, at No4 a shepherd who was also the milk deliveryman.

Geoff's dad, known as Perps, was chiefly a horseman, in charge of a team of working shire horses that did all the heavy work about the farm. He loved his horses, gave them names and carefully tended them. Geoff remembers in particular the horses named Heather and Flower, a mare and stallion respectively that worked well together. The horses were large chunky animals. Heather was two - tone grey and Flower was chestnut - brown and black. Both had flowing white 'socks'.

FARM LIFE

This way of life holds great satisfaction and pleasure to those reared into it but there are keenly sad times too, especially concerning the animals. The stallion, Flower, with a potential life span of 30 years managed about only half that time He started with what is termed itchy withers. The withers are the equivalent of the nape of the neck in humans; it is where the thick collar rests on the horse. It is covered with leather with flannel underneath but there is pressure and some friction however well fitting the collar may be. This area in Flower became sore; despite ointment, medicine and injections the sore got worse and broke out into a weeping wound. It was an anxious time. Man and beast working closely together form a powerful bond and mutual affection grows. The animal lost interest in eating and quickly, within weeks, became skin and bone - Flower had developed cancer.

The inevitable happened, Flower had to be humanely killed. Father and son wept together. They watched as the humane killer was applied to the forehead by the vet - Flower collapsed immediately with a sickening clatter on to the cobbled yard. And that was the inglorious end of a loyal old friend and indeed, colleague.

The pathetically emaciated body of Flower sprawled there on the cobbles, a far cry from that former sturdy, willing horse with rippling muscles and alert eyes. Looking back, Geoff feels that the horse was allowed to suffer too long.

We shudder as we remember the horrors of the foot-and mouth disease early this 21st Century - and more recent scares - a tragic time for both animal and farmer.

Like humans, the new horse had to learn his job and the old and new horses had to become accustomed to each other, and horses too have different temperaments.

DAD (PERCY)

Percy spent long hours ploughing, sowing, preparing and reaping the land in all weathers. The winter temperatures were severe when his hands were often gnarled and deeply fissured with open sores - tough hard-working hands. Even with gloves the hands suffered. And even Dad's leisure hours were industriously spent on productive hobbies, ever working to provide for his family. He grew vegetables in his garden allotment at the rear of their terraced cottage.

He also reared hens, linnets and canaries in a patch across the back lane. In winter they were brought into the back kitchen on to a shelf; they were beautiful singers. He would put them outside on mild days. He would acquire his first linnets with a very cunning ploy; Geoff remembers his father moving by degrees a nest of linnets that originated in the hedgerow in front of the cottage. The whole distance moved would be as much as 100yards, moving it on a daily basis. He would patiently wait until the chicks had all hatched to do this. All the while the parents would be returning to the nest to feed the young, guided by their insistent chirping. The last move would be to place the nest complete with growing fledglings in a cage hanging on a hook on the cottage wall. He placed the nest close to the cage bars so that the parent birds continued feeding them through the bars. No doubt he sold the birds that he did not require.

Two young magpies were caught by one of Geoff's school friends and he kept them in a home made wooden cage. The boy taught them to speak, just simple phrases. Probably because there were two of them they did not die of stress and loneliness.

One sad morning a sorry sight greeted the family - they awoke to find dad's canaries and linnets, at least half-a-dozen breeding pairs, dead in the kitchen; dad had forgotten to move them for the night into the warm living room. Perhaps it had been an unpredictably cold night. Poor dad was smitten with grief compounded with guilt and the anger that accompanies guilt.

In the kitchen, he hatched the eggs of his hens plus those of wild or farm geese, moorhens and ducks. He used a cotton wool lined wooden box near the fire range that was rotated to keep even warmth to hatch the eggs. To enhance the family menu still further he would bring rabbits home and the eggs of various wild fowl etc. Geoff and his mother assisted in some of this hands-on food production as Dad's weekly wage was the equivalent to only £1 50p up until the War.

Always looking for ways to stretch the tight family budget, Dad discovered that a full stream actually ran under the house where trout were seen to be swimming! There was no cellar so access to this stream was managed by taking up the floor boards in the living room, thus in the comfort of his home, quietly poised with rod and bait he would successfully poach trout!

As a countryman he had all kinds of skills and knowledge related to country living - skills sadly being lost as the years go by as machinery takes over. Fortunately today there are heritage centres that demonstrate the trades of a past rural life; however many skills have been lost and forgotten.

Things were tough, the working day used up most of the daylight hours, but Geoff's Father had that deep at-oneness with his life, his work and environment that you find in those whose hearts beat in rhythm with the pulse of nature and are in tune with the ebb and flow of the seasons.

~

Man - and woman - is made up of the dust - the elements of the earth as taught in the Holy Bible, in Genesis Chapter 2 verse 7, and as science has since discovered. So there is a special deep satisfaction and spiritual dimension within the soul of one who works the soil, especially in association with animals.

Boredom does not exist in the experience of one who is steeped in the magic of the earth's productive powers and fruitfulness, he/she is sensitive to the changing moods of the weather, anticipates the steady progression of the seasons, and prepares for the changing tasks heralded by the signs of the changes. Tragically, the economic changes and pressures of modern life have resulted in the suicide of many farmers of our generation as they experience a steady eroding of rural community life as a viable lifestyle.

~

AN AFFINITY WITH NATURE

Within Geoff grew a love of country life. He developed a listening ear and an alert eye for the ways of nature and a bonding with animals under the quiet but powerful influence of his simple country father, the strong man of hard work, the steady, reliable, plodding fellow of few words and hidden emotion.

His mother who was a lively social person was not so enamoured with the life, as the unfolding of Geoff's story will reveal!

Geoff was the youngest of four children who were born in quick succession; perhaps they came too quickly for his mother, for sadly, she became unhappy with her lot.... Things were to change, drastically...and after all, she was a townie.

CHAPTER TWO

An Awakening

GEOFF THE FREE SPIRIT -

Geoff was a happy wander in the woods and fields for much of his early childhood in Hatfield and later in S Wales. He loved expeditions of discovery around the rich countryside, enjoying and learning about the flora and fauna at first hand and he became entranced by the creatures that live in and around water!

He would bring home specimens of insect creatures in a matchbox and after a short while release them in the garden. He loved the grasshopper, but beasties like frogs, toads and mice he would often pocket to bring home and wondered why they did not remain there at his convenience! He became the constant source of daytime nightmares for his mother and sister who would discover these creatures in various corners of the cottage! His mother would jump, scream, holler and squeal! Gasping she would plead with her son to stop bringing home this "Ugh!" wild life! But to no avail! It was a grand and inspiring obsession!

Oh! Those fascinating ponds, marshes, copses and hedgerows, all teeming with wonderful, intriguing, often beautiful, life. .Now all gone - concreted over - built on, in the soulless, pitiless name of progress.

~

The curiosity of young children can be described as pure for they enjoy a natural excitable delight in the marvels of nature as they relish their voyage of discovery - things that later, most of us are repulsed by. They are not hampered by the feelings of revulsion that often develop, probably passed on by the attitudes and responses of the adults around them.

Sadly, that initial spontaneous joy and wonder in natural things is subsequently spoiled, replaced by wariness and fear, which is of course the development of the necessary instinct of self-preservation.

~

Exploring was Geoff's favourite pastime; he spent a lot of time on his own roaming the countryside, even when small. One summer's day, at not much older than six years, something extraordinary happened.

He was lazing around in the grass at the time, lying on his back watching the scudding clouds changing colour and shape. Simultaneously he was listening to the bird chorus with the constant hum of a multi-choir of varied flying insects - subtly breathing in the scents of the countryside when something stirred deep within him. It was a shift into a different level of consciousness.

He rolled over and started studying what he found, stirring the soil and parting the meadow plants. Great activity was going on in the grass The more he moved the grasses the more he saw of the many busy insects living in their own world-in-miniature, scurrying about their business of living. He became aware of the myriad intricate patterns of life - above, on, and below ground. He thought of that boundless world high in the skies - too remote! - too immeasurable! - Even for the imagination. Suddenly his small world expanded into a glorious vastness of wonderfully interweaving systems like millions of cog- wheels working together to operate an immense and complex machine. Oh the mystery of it all! He was transfixed – fascinated!

With awesome revelation within his soul this new consciousness made him aware that there were *Worlds Within a World within a world.* It dawned on him that there were hidden spheres of life expressing glorious variety amazingly dependent on one another and in which humans have a very special place

Obviously he was too young to be thinking or feeling in words - he was not applying any sense of logic or special knowledge - his own tender, innocent and unsullied spirit was simply resonating and making a connexion with, that great Spirit of All Being - the Spirit Pulse in the Heart of Creation. His young mind at an instinctive level suddenly realised that all these beautifully balanced, organised and interlocking expressions of life had to be created by an outstanding intelligent Being, a Being that we call God.

He had experienced *an awakening* in his spirit

Up to this point and in fact through his entire upbringing he received no religious teaching or bias of any sort, except for Scripture stories at school.

His mother neither expressed nor showed any religious conviction except that she was superstitious and followed the superstitious rituals that have their root in paganism. Superstition is a basic awareness of *The Other World,* but sadly, common practices are based on fear involving routines that might be called 'safety' rites - like not crossing knives or walking under a ladder as these may bring bad luck; whereas conversely, the emphasis of the Christian Faith is on confidence, peace and hope!

However, unexpectedly, when Geoff left home to go overseas in the Army - very lovingly and tenderly, his Mother gave him a Rosary! The cross was inscribed with the words -'souvenir' and

'Lourdes' - the beads were a dark grey/brown. Surely, this gift was a simple act of faith or, unsaid prayer. Rather regrettably, he knows nothing of its history but it is a special keepsake.

This *awakening* was the birth of a simple non-theological, non-religious, untaught faith in a Supreme Being; a wondrous realisation - a watershed in Geoff's life that quietly and subtly influenced his attitudes in life and towards life thereon. This enlightenment would be the first intimation that deep within the soul of his being there existed a *world within a world...* **or sense within the senses...** But many years would elapse, even 60 years, before he would have yet another powerful stirring of this, his deeper nature.

What had arisen within him was a 'knowing' of an unseen world of reality that comes from the sense of the spirit, which is more likely to happen spontaneously in those whose lives are lived close to the earth - conscious of the rhythms, seasons and hum of Nature.

He kept this experience to himself, an experience that went far beyond the constraints and inadequacies of mere words anyhow! ...He did not speak of it until *decades* later.

~

But these other-worldly experiences are rarely spoken of by those who experience them for they are so special that the recipients cannot comprehend that others may have had the same spiritual 'quickening' or elevation. Certainly in our material Western culture, spiritual experiences and visions are not spoken about for fear of one being labelled a crank, superstitious or somewhat unhinged!

~

UNDERSTANDING WHAT HAPPENED TO GEOFF

With others as with Geoff, the amazing spheres of Nature, the adaptability of its creatures and the delicately balanced complexity of the universe can give rise to an inner revelation that is *other-worldly* to point us to God, and something is birthed *within.*

When with awe and wonder we consider all the many mediums of life on this planet - and the relationship of the heavenly bodies in space - and we meditate on the ever- moving miracle of life we realise that there is a universal bonding element which is spiritual in nature. It is the stuff of *another world that resonates with a world within deep in the core- heart of the human being. The stuff is spiritual - not seen but sensed*

As we ponder in awe with the tool of this new awareness, the *world within* strengthens and we come to realise that we hold a significant place in the wheel of life in the whole of this incredible creation. Even the rocks have a life! - They are constantly being shaped and eroded by the action of wind and waves.

A new knowledge and conviction grows. It is that we are not simply a tiny blob of flesh/matter in a soulless planet repetitively orbiting in measureless space - randomly populated with evolving life forms, existing simply because they have passed one of Nature's rigorous laws - 'the survival of the fittest'.

The doors to so many of levels of life and creation, hitherto hidden, have been opened to us in our generation, by sophisticated devices - by space travel and the power of magnification in the use of special microscopes and telescopes. Yet, sadly today, people, especially young people have lost the sense of being part of the Great Continuum of Life, have lost the awareness of the miracle of re-creation and regeneration in which we humans have a special role. For too many of our human species in our time, have become distanced from the life that is all around; largely because we have surrounded ourselves with concrete, high walls and other spiritually barren man-made structures that even blot out the risings and settings of the sun. Another factor is that someone lays a claim to every square foot of land; there was the time when parcels of 'spare' ground where children could play, were dotted around towns and villages. Where these wild places were, you will now find a building, a road, or - a car!

No longer do we sense that we are creatures of the earth – rooted, supported and sustained by the earth - composed of the elements of the earth - water, salt, calcium iron and all the other elements that make up the human body. The words of the traditional Christian funeral service as the lifeless body is committed to the ground, reminds us of this, as science has discovered - that - physically at any rate - we are - 'dust to dust' that is - earth to earth.

The avid gardener sees the soil of the earth as much more than 'dust'- rather, he/she is conscious of its mysterious life giving power and becomes entranced and hooked by the manipulation of its life emerging processes, watching in delight and wonder as plants develop and unfold day by day.

The feel of the soil can be a spiritual experience! Geoff has been a keen gardener for most of his life but in the later years he took outdoor work for health reason; in the years before retirement was self employed as a general and landscape gardener He had been a smoker from his teens until the age of 47years and had worked amongst diesel and petrol fumes for many years. A legacy of this was the onset of periodic bronchial asthma.

Children see magic in the world around, there is beauty and wonder surrounding us of which they are keenly and often rapturously aware and will squeal in delight at the discovery of the simple earthworm for they will pick it up with no fear, even carrying it to the mouth! A little child can lead us! if we will slow down, tune in to, and share his/her world!

This inner spiritual dimension is what places us in a completely different rank of species to any other living creature. What other creature can be overwhelmed with the sense of awe and wonder?

We, of the human species, uniquely, are able to put two and two together and come up with five, or is it seven the perfect number! because the 'sense' of our spirit, *our inner world,* tunes into *that other world (of spiritual reality) within a world* - the latter being this physical world. Thus we realise by the sensitivity of our inner spirit that there is much more to life than we can perceive with the five senses.

Tragically, extended pain and injustice can blunt the human spirit, and rationality often overtakes to block the subtle promptings and wisdom of the spirit.

A Magic Moment In Early Spring

It was an early day in Spring, I tripped along with jaunty swing!
The air was clear and fresh and bright, I felt a glow, my heart was light!
The land enjoyed a sun-kissed day, the frost & snow now passed away,
A longed for sight of spring reborn - the stir of life in hedge and lawn. .

New life was humming in the air - A time when earth seems void of care,
I felt the vibrance all around, as plants renewing claimed the ground.
The sky above my head was blue; caressing breezes round me blew,
Forever - Spring dawns to amaze! To wrench the grasp of Winter's days.

In joy my eyes skimmed pastures fair, I praised my Lord's Creative flair!
Confirming Hope in Heaven sublime, a moment rare transcended Time
For magic did my heart ensnare, as thrilling chimes echoed the air!
For suddenly! The hillside rang! - A trill of bells! - A robin sang!

CHAPTER THREE

SAD CHANGES

THE FLIGHT TO NEWPORT MONMOUTHSHIRE, SOUTH WALES

I MENTIONED EARLIER THAT ALL was not well with Geoff's mother whom he loved dearly. They had taken an occasional lodger, Bill, when as a lorry driver he was delivering in the area. No doubt this helped with the finances. Bill's home was in Newport, Monmouthshire, S Wales. A relationship grew and in 1931, dramatically, especially for that era of loyalty to marriage whatever the cost, Mum left with this man, taking with her the youngest child, Geoffrey, 4yrs and the eldest child Joyce, 9yrs. Left behind were the two middle children -Tom, 5+yrs and Joan 8yrs. Geoff's Mum left a note on the kitchen table; it must have come as a terrible shock to faithful, quietly contented Dad.

They made their escape in a rather slow-moving steam-powered transport lorry, the vehicle Bill used as a long distance lorry driver. It had solid rubber wheels, hardly comfort travel for a journey from Hertfordshire to Newport in South Wales!

Geoff was not feeling well; it was a miserable trip. When they eventually arrived, Geoff was found to be suffering from the Mumps, swollen neck glands! Even worse - it was his birthday, his fifth! Leaving all that he had ever known, on his birthday! - Some celebration!

For most of the following years they frequently moved address, in rented rooms, often in a shared house, sometimes they had the luxury of a whole house, rented. Left behind were the surrounding fields. However, he found his beloved ponds, riverbanks and wild places around Newport that helped the settling- in process. Again, most of these exploring places are no more today.

Naturally, life had its advantages and disadvantages in the new environment

A cruel humiliation - Geoff remembers a very humiliating and upsetting experience at around the tender and sensitive age of seven:

Geoff's terraced house ran at right angles to a street down which they looked, from their house front windows. The people of this street had prepared a street party to celebrate a national event. There was no such party in his street because there were few residential properties.

Street parties were quite common before and after the War.

Geoff was sitting on their garden wall looking enviously at the party in full swing.

A woman who lived in that street approached him, with a welcoming smile she said,

"Would you like to join the party? Bring your plate, cup and saucer."

"Yes please! "

Geoff went off home for the required crockery that was all-blue pottery. He walked back down the street in happy anticipation and the woman joined him.

"I'll find you a place on a bench." He sat down.

"I'll get you a cup of tea!" Which she did. "Help yourself to the food!"

There was a colourful feast for the eye and happy anticipation of enjoying the goodies. There were sandwiches, rolls, cakes, jellies etc. She moved away to serve the other children.

Then another stern-looking woman approached him,

"What are you doing here? You don't belong in this street! ... Go home!"

Geoff felt mortified; he rose and departed, feeling heart broken. He never had chance even to enjoy his tea, under his breath he muttered,

"I won't drink your mouldy tea!" He poured it down a drain on his way home, tears falling.

Mum asked, "What's the matter?" - She promised him a lovely tea to compensate.

But it did little to heal the wound of senseless rejection!

This incident prompted me to muse on the *'us and them'* complex

~

Deep in the nature of the beast are primal instincts such as the instincts of herd, clan and/or territory. Homo Sapiens share these deep instincts with the animal kingdom that is - facets of the more fundamental instinct of self-preservation. Most animals react with suspicion when confronted with the unfamiliar because of assumed threat or danger. The defence of safety and the need to preserve offspring and assets prompts all humans to resist imposed changes that outsiders threaten to bring. It is essentially an us-and-them complex and very observable in children as well as most animals.

When leaders, social planners and government fail to acknowledge the-nature-of-the-beast common to all living creatures, well, mammals certainly, and try to educate these instincts out of people, they will fail. Social problems arise springing from resentment and hidden fear which are tough to eradicate

Fear of the strange and unfamiliar, is common to all. So is the tendency of humans to think that those who look and sound different are somehow inferior, to be despised or feared! This is an irrational but basic part of life. Much human behaviour is not sifted and checked by reason.

There will always be those who fail in bringing their more basic reactions and feelings under the control of rational thinking, for the common good. The woman who drove out Geoff from the party was not using her rational mind but rather acting from deep instincts that say -

'You are an outsider therefore you have no right to join in with *us*!'

Sadly, how demeaning is this attitude! Geoff shrivelled inside himself.

To bring stable peace and cohesion to disparate groups, who look, sound or behave differently from each other because they are from strikingly different backgrounds, in *some* situations can be as difficult to establish as cutting wood against the grain! But thank God people can adapt and change for the common good.

~

DEATH BY DIPHTHERIA

Deaths of children by the childhood diseases that are now prevented by inoculation tragically were not uncommon.

Geoff was playing with his sister and several other children in the back garden of his home when a 6yrs old girl with a bandage round her neck shared her pop with several others - drinking from her bottle. Some days later Geoff, his sister Joyce and the other young playmates started being feverish with a painful sore throat. Joyce caused great concern as she became seriously ill but survived. Her throat was painted with "some blue stuff" (perhaps -gentian violet for it was used as an applied medication in those days) They learned that the little girl, generous with her pop, had also given away her sore throat which turned out to be the dreadful and deadly disease of diphtheria. There are different types but it can cause suffocation by a membrane forming across the throat.

A little later came the awful news that the little girl had become seriously ill leading to death.. Geoff feels that this was one of several occasions when he came near to death.

BACK TO ROEGREEN

About five years later when Geoff was 10yrs, Mum decided to return home, no doubt missing and feeling guilty about her two middle children left with their father.

They travelled by train and taxi. Geoff's Dad was expecting them. When they met up Geoff smelt whiskey on his father's breath - it was a tense meeting. His parents did not resume sleeping together in the marital bed.

THE NIGHTMARISH CHRISTMAS OF 1937

Within a few months the Christmas season had arrived which normally, was a wonderful time spent with Mum's parents in a generously sized house between North Clapham and Brixton, London. The grandparents would pull out all the stops to make these occasions special and joyous with generous presents waiting for the children.

This particular Christmas would have been a little different because the grandparents had recently moved to a Brixton house in Winslade Road so it was here that the family spent Christmas - but without Mum who was not invited!

Not long after this the grandparents moved again because of an unexploded bomb in the Brixton area. They went to New Malden, Surrey to live in their son's house. The son had moved to Leeds because of a job promotion to become bank Manager.

Tragically, this Christmas was to be so *dreadfully* different - for Mum.

Neither Lill's husband nor her parents had forgiven her the adultery and disloyalty. Her parents did not welcome her that Christmas; she had to stay behind, alone in the quiet farm cottage, no doubt painfully listening to the celebrations of the neighbours on either side. How different the lives of every member of that family would have been if her folks had truly celebrated the Spirit of Christmas with the heart of love that Christmas teaches in the Love-gift of God in the sending of his Son Jesus to earth. He sacrificed his glorious home in heaven to come to earth, and he too was to be rejected and suffer many things!

Mum had a heart of gold, straight and caring, basically a good woman; can we in imagination visit Geoff's poor Mum, sitting, poignantly alone, tears streaming down her face, shaking with heart-broken sobs, feeling confused, damned and rejected....And haunted ... taunted, by memories from the past, of warm, loving, joyful Christmases, exchanging presents surrounded by her laughing excited children...

Retracing footsteps - It is no wonder that Mum soon escaped back to Newport. Her new common-law husband must have been a generous hearted bloke to receive her back for he had returned to his family and so it meant making a new home together, again.

~

Tragically, it often happens that the things that attract a couple to each other in the first place, and opposites attract, are the things that later develop into a wedge that drives a couple apart. That self centred part of us all, secretly wants to pair with someone who shares all our interests, aspirations, values and beliefs, a kind of mirror image of self. But marriage is a partnership where people should blend their unique individual characters with appreciation and respect for the differences between them; to blend the two halves into a rich composite whole. But the required level of self-denial and bending that is needed by one in some relationships becomes a burden too great. The strain on flawed human love causes partnerships to collapse.

~

MOTHER RETURNS TO NEWPORT A SECOND TIME - WITHOUT GEOFF

On this trip back to Newport her daughter Joyce accompanied Mum. But -

"I want to be with my Dad!" Said Geoff,

His sister Joan, then 15yrs, had been 'the woman of the house' looking after Dad as best she could. She was now working at De Haviland's Aeroplane factory, painting camouflage on the planes, for this was wartime. But now she had the added responsibility of her brother.

Poor little urchin boy - Ah! Soon, Geoff was living like an urchin boy: thin, with unwashed clothes and long tousled hair. He went to school again locally - that is, he went once and refused to go again! They were doing decimals and he had learnt nothing about them. It was a shaming experience so he vowed never to go again! And he didn't! Geoff had already had the unnerving experience of attending three schools in Newport - five schools in all. He was little more than 10yrs old!

Oh yes, the school 'Bobby' - the School Board man, came to the house and made stern threatening noises at his Dad about being sent to Court. In those days the school 'Bobby' was somebody to be feared and action was normally taken; but for some strange reason his file must have been lost or pushed to one side. The School Board man was never seen again. His dad gave him one warning.... And that was the last on the subject of education!

But, Geoff could not go on living like that.

Just once, Mum with sister Joyce had managed to visit him, their unsuccessful mission being to persuade him to return to Newport. The rendezvous was a local cafe to which Geoff cycled. He arrived bearing gifts! He proudly presented Mum with 6 eggs laid by his own two chickens! .

After eighteen months Geoff got fed up with his way of life. As time went by he was missing his mother - her love, care and not least, her appetizing and steaming hot meals! He was feeling more and more lonely and generally feeling like a lost soul. So he wrote to her and she wrote back arranging for him to be picked up by Bill, his step-father, at noon on a particular day, perhaps a Friday when Bill would be on his journey home from the South of England to S Wales. Dad was not informed of the plan, but before he left Geoff wrote a letter and left it propped up on the mantelpiece to be found when Dad came home from work. This must have been the third heart lurching "Goodbye." letter that Percy had read.

LEAVING DAD TO JOIN MOTHER IN NEWPORT

On the day of travel, Geoff fixed his few meagre worldly possessions on a 'bogey' cart. The items included his precious all-purpose knife and red alarm clock with bell on top. His beloved clock ticked noisily amongst his things!

The cart was a homemade contraption made of a set of pram wheels, a plank with wooden box on top between the front and back wheels. Strong string or rope was fixed to the front wheel-axle and the cart was guided with the feet and braked by the feet scraping the ground!

The place of pick-up was 'The New Fiddle' about a mile from home. Whilst he was walking to the Inn a casual pal of his approached from the opposite direction!

"Where are you going?" The friend queried.

"I'm going away, don't tell anyone!" Replied Geoff, shrewdly omitting a mention of his mother.

"I won't." His friend assured him.

He reached The New Fiddle and settled down to wait…and he waited ...and waited …became thirsty and hungry, he had no packed lunch...Time ticks by slowly at that age ...His heart pounded in fear! What if he had to go back home? How would Dad feel, especially about the planning - nay - the plotting that had gone on behind his back? Dad *would* understand, there would be no physical chastisement, just a dull, silent, defeated resignation.

~

Poor loyal, often dog-tired farmer's man. Surely he would wonder how he had failed - felt that he had done his very best, but it wasn't enough ... worked his guts out ... for what?

And if your*very* best won't do, and you are discarded for another, what a dark, soul destroying place to arrive at on life's road! – It is a deep pit of despair in which many have foundered. For some without hope and faith no way through is seen.

~

Anxiety mounted - and hunger as Geoff contemplated his apparent plight, especially at the thought of being spotted by an adult who knew his family. Noon was well past; Bill had been delayed. Then, what a relief! He heard and spotted Bill's lorry down the main road. - It was 2.15pm.

Soon they were on their way, then stopping for refreshments. After a journey lasting at least seven hours - no motorways then - it was dark and well on in the evening when they finally arrived, chilled and weary. The cab of the lorry was cold.

And once again Geoff arrived in Newport - unwell!

This time it was the 'flu that put him to bed for some days.

It was 1940 when Geoff arrived in Newport for the second time to live with his mother, Bill and sister Joyce. Bill was frequently away from home transporting heavy goods, but an amicable relationship grew. After Joyce married Geoff lived with his mother and Bill until he married himself aged 26yrs.

Despite missing the chance of making friends at school in Newport - as he never went! happily, Geoff soon made friends with a neighbour's boy, Bobby, and others later. For both boys an interest in girls soon developed.

His family for a while lived opposite the Athletic Grounds - the home of The Black and Tans Newport Rugby Club. Geoff and his new friends would go in and upturn the flat wooden benches to slide down the supporter stands, that is, until the grounds-man caught them! In running away Geoff fell and badly hurt himself, maybe that's why he received a mild slap only rather than the customary good hiding for such an offence! Normally, the police would have been called in. His friend got away!

Time passed quite pleasantly as he got on with his 'mission' in life - wandering and exploring rural Newport; and to make a little cash he sold the popular comics of the day - the 'Dandy' and 'Beano' for one old penny each, until the time that he was offered his first job.

CHAPTER FOUR

Horses Humans And Others

WORKING LIFE STARTS FOR GEOFF - AT THE AGE OF 13YRS

Geoff had not attended school since before his eleventh birthday and as time trickled by he became eager to start employment. It had to be a situation that did not vex his free spirit. He soon found that even if he liked a particular job he could not cope with being shut up between four walls, he came to realise that he was much happier being self-employed; well, in a kind of way he had spent a good part of his young life being his own 'boss' so a pattern had been set!

LEARNING THE HAIRDRESSING TRADE

He was offered the job of lather boy in a barber's shop with the chance of making a career.

Characteristically, after more than two years, Geoff felt imprisoned in the four walls of a back room with no view except the towering wall of the railway embankment and the only touch of nature was a Virginia Creeper climbing up this wall! Autumn turned it into a beautiful vibrant red.

His employer was sympathetic, he promised to watch out for other job opportunities for Geoff. He heard of a vacancy in a motorbike factory, which stripped down used bikes and reconditioned them, many came from the Army, some from accidents.

So Geoff threw in the barber's towel - so to speak!

THE MOTOR BIKE FACTORY

Atco - The firm previously made Atco Motor Mowers.

Geoff started in the large stores department that housed all bike parts and related tools.

At the young age of sixteen he was teased, as was the custom. A mechanic would ask him to bring from store a packet of blue ignition sparks! Geoff fell for it of course and would obligingly go off into the stores interior on a fool's errand - until he stopped in his tracks as he heard a raucous guffaw behind him - sheepishly he would slouch back to the counter!

On different occasions he was asked to provide:- a rubber hammer, a rubber chisel, a foo-foo valve, and a skyhook - to hang the bikes on!

In only two weeks Geoff felt imprisoned again!

He was offered a job on the assembly line - the only available vacancy. His job was stripping down bikes into parts; the parts were placed in boxes and sent to the degreasing cleaning section. Bent frames would be straightened and other parts would be repaired or replaced to build a reconditioned bike on the assembly line.

Geoff became quite skilled and rather enjoyed the work especially as he realised that he was building up muscle in the regular lifting of the bikes, which he managed solo; he disassembled four an hour. He handled all the makes of the day - Matchless, Norton, Ariel, BSA and (American) Indian - to name a few. Then he graduated to the assembly line. The firm employed both boys and girls

Generally, it was dirty, greasy work with the hazard of air pollution by the cleaning chemicals and paint spray. Some bikes came from the Army Regiments and would be sprayed with khaki green.

After about a month, Geoff and another lad took a bike for a run that Geoff had completed, working on the end of the assembly line. It was his task to actually start the engines. It was strictly forbidden to attempt to ride them, but Geoff, with his pal on the pillion, zoomed off outside in the lunch break and rode around the block - of mostly houses.

Someone, an elderly employee, reported both of them and they were suspended for a month. It was unrealistic to hang around without pay for so long - so that job bit the dust!

ALL BRITISH CARRIERS AND HORSES- (ABC) NEWPORT

The next firm that Geoff worked for were distributors of foodstuffs and heavy haulage such as coils of steel, angled iron and steel girders etc. He was on the loading bay to start with. Then a vacancy arose for horse and cart delivery driver, supplying local shops and factories with food and other goods; the money was better. (Rationing was tight during this period of the war) Geoff applied for the job and he went for interview. He was taken on because of his farm animal experience.

He thought to himself, "Freedom at last in the outdoors! - **And** - with a horse!"

The delivery round however, was proving too much to cover because Jim, the horse that had been supplied was very slow, and stubborn. The foreman arranged for an exchange with a horse from Cardiff.

On the day of the exchange, Geoff set off riding Jim, apart from a sack, bare backed. On the way they crossed a road bridge over a main railway line. Suddenly a train passed under the bridge with a great noise and clouds of steam. Both horse and driver were startled.

Jim panicked and ran sideways across the road into the side of an oncoming loaded lorry promptly knocking Geoff off into the middle of the road. He fell heavily on his side and sat up gingerly feeling a sharp pain in his left side; Jim galloped off down the road with a speed Geoff had never witnessed before! The lorry was disappearing having failed to stop!

Geoff caught up with Jim some 0.25mls further on, nonchalantly munching grass at the roadside! Stupidly, Geoff felt angry at the horse that had shown quite a different temperament on this occasion because normally, he had come over as a very placid, solid animal. Had Geoff hit him in temper he certainly would have come off worst!

Geoff walked beside the horse for much of the remainder of the way. His chest was hurting, as he had been badly bruised with a cigarette case that he carried in his chest pocket.

The plan was to meet half way with a man bringing up the new horse but Geoff was late and the other man had come much further towards Newport than had been arranged. The man, whom he had never met before, was non-too pleased.

Geoff had got up later than he should which did not help matters.

Geoff meets his partner - Billie the horse! - What a happy meeting! What a difference! And what a lovely working partner Billie turned out to be. He was a gelding (A male horse that has been castrated to be trained to work - Horses would be too wild and disobedient to handle otherwise) He was several hands taller than Jim and was a lovely dappled silver grey. He had a gorgeous long silver mane and tail that had been groomed well for that first meeting.

Billie was quicker on his hooves and had a willing, cheeky nature. They were soon great pals.

Geoff took pride in the appearance of horse, harness and cart. He saw to it that the brassware was always gleaming; it was a weekly task, and sometimes he would blacken his hooves. Rain caused frustration because it would take off the shine.

Geoff's senior colleague Bert taught him the job - taught him how to act when a horse stops in his tracks to relieve himself. The horse driver has to quickly change position otherwise he would be drenched! Bert also instructed him to nonchalantly whistle whilst the horse was stationery answering Nature's call, this could take minutes and urine would pour like a stream into the gutter. The whistle has the effect of calming the horse who realises that his driver is happy to wait for him. And afterwards, the horse will automatically move off.

Geoff was taught to walk very closely round the back of a horse or keep well away because an angry or frightened horse is likely to kick. He kicks with one hoof several feet backwards, such a kick can kill, especially a child.

A cow, on the other hand, kicks *forward* with his back legs - this was a hazard for the milking maids of old who were also at risk from getting lashed on the face and head, with a nasty stinging wet and foul tail!

Geoff and Bert took it in turns on Sundays and bank holidays to go into the stables to tend the two horses. Bert drove a mare called Kitty. She was a gentle-natured horse, a large chestnut brown. Sadly she had a problem - she came from London and had suffered from the noise of air raids and the metallic clatter of shrapnel bouncing on the metal stable roof, her nerves were affected. Any loud noise, especially a bang, would terrify her -she would literally dance on the spot and shake. If she were in the shafts of the cart, the whole outfit would rattle, frighteningly! Thunderstorms also evoked terror.

Billie was not able to manage as heavy a load as Jim. The maximum that he could manage would be up to two ton. Sometimes the load on the return journey would be too heavy, such as tins of paint; this would cause Billie to slip when pulling over the River Bridge in Newport. To assist grip, Geoff, with the aid of a hammer would bang into the open ends of the horseshoes, anti-slip pegs. The pegs, which would be pulled out with pliers on the crown of the bridge, acted as a kind of a heel for the horse for extra leverage to pull up inclines. Horses lean forward when pulling a heavy load.

Sometimes the foreman stocked the cart with a too-heavy load. Geoff would sometimes help Billie by pulling a rope attached to the front of the cart. Man and horse would heave together!

Billie got to know the delivery stops and especially where he would receive treats. The best for treats was a works' canteen; he would cheekily put his head in the door, cart behind. Everyone was supposed to halt at the works gate entrance where the gateman was lodged, but Billie, with his mind on treats, would refuse to halt! The lodge-man got used to this and would laugh. Billie knew when the places for treats were looming - his pace would quicken! Scribona cakes were among the delivery goods.

Billie had many mischievous tricks. He would tease Geoff and would impishly step on his feet; when he was being groomed he would lean against Geoff trapping him against the stall sides, arms pinned up in the air. Sometimes Geoff would be lifted right off the ground as Billie grasped him with his huge teeth by the pads of his coat!

Geoff arrived every morning at around 8am, the first job being to feed and water the horses. The two creatures in horsy language would joyously greet him with their -

'Good morning! Nice to see yer!" - a chorus of hearty neighing and the toss of two heads!

Rough justice - On one bank holiday, Geoff went to the yard to give Billie some exercise and feed. The foreman was doing some work in his office, unbeknown to Geoff. He untied the horse and led him out of the stable. Once released, Billie ran around the yard in jubilation; it was a very large yard off which were the storehouses and lorry loading bays.

The foreman - nicknamed Fatty Bennet because he was short and tubby - came out of his office in a state of alarm having spotted the horse charging around.

"Geoff! Your horse has escaped!" -

"Yes, I've let him go free for a bit of exercise!"

"But he looks very dangerous to me!"

The horse looked lively indeed - shaking his head and swishing his glorious tail, glad to be free! From time to time he would trot up to Geoff raising his head and neighing his thanks. Then he would quickly pivot around and gallop off again, tail swishing wildly.

But the horse heard the foreman's voice echoing in the shed and galloped towards him. Geoff in devilment shouted a warning.

"Look out! He'll have you - for putting those heavy loads on him - he's remembered!"

Bennet puffed up the steps to his office in fright. *"Don't* do that again when *I'm* here!"

Geoff chuckled inwardly.

"Farewell Billie ... my old pal! You've served me well!"

This job came to an end when Geoff was called up into the Army -1944 - the war was not yet won. With not a little twinge of sadness, he had to say a sad farewell, not only to friends and family but also to his fantastic horse-work-mate, Billie.

Later when Geoff was in the Army he learned by letter that things had improved for the horses; they were being taken to fields to graze for the one and half-day weekends and were better for it. But the current driver reported that Billie was always difficult to catch in the field after his weekend of freedom!

Geoff did not want Army life; he tried to 'dodge the column' by being classed as doing a 'reserved occupation' or essential job, but the ploy failed.

Geoff's army days are recounted in the chapter - 'On His Majesties Service.'

LIFE AFTER SERVING HIS MAJESTY

Coming home in 1948, demobbed after serving in the Army there was the question of employment but Geoff was not penniless because he had carefully saved from his pay.

His sister Joyce was working for a catering firm as a cashier; Mrs Hatton owned the firm; stories involving her appear in the chapter 'It must have been an angel'. Joyce told her brother that Mrs Hatton, a widow, was looking for a chauffer to take her around on business and personal trips. He took the job and for 2yrs loved it but poor pay, five pounds weekly, prompted him to look elsewhere.

Following this job he became a taxi driver for a local firm to improve his earnings. Some stories from this era are recounted in the introduction of this book.

An assortment of jobs followed.

STARTING A BUSINESS

Already married, Geoff, in his thirties in 1959 bought shop premises in Malpas Newport; he was working as a car-sales man at the time and hoped later to develop his own business.

A year later he met up with two old work mates who were in business in the car trade but using poor premises, they offered to take Geoff as a full partner to establish a new firm in Geoff's premises calling the new company, Monmouthshire Motor Cycles. They undertook to pay the mortgage and rent of £22 monthly out of the profits. They adapted the premises and things started to do well and in building up the stock, selling scooters that currently were all the rage. These included the Italian Vespa, Lambretta, and German makes. Also they sold the 3-wheeler bubble cars etc

The business should have prospered but for two reasons it hit trouble: -

One of the partners developed polio from which he never fully recovered. It left him weak for the rest of his life and he never recovered sufficiently to cope with a normal job. The other two carried him but it put a strain on the business and sadly they had to relinquish him as a partner after about 9months when he was bought out.

Then Geoff found that his remaining partner was not pulling his weight so the business folded after much adaptation work had been carried out on the premises. It was a great disappointment.

The curl of smoke - During the time that Geoff and his partners ran the motorbike shop, he and his wife Jan lived in the flat above. What seems a very hazardous arrangement to our present day safety-conscious minds, the open coal fire had an original wooden Adam style surround with a tiled inside border and there was a small hearth set in the wooden floor boards of the living room. The hearth was edged with a wooden fender. There was a recess at both sides of the fireplace.

Geoff was relaxing in a chair placed partly in the left alcove to the side of the fire when he saw a curl of smoke arising from the skirting board in the alcove. Jan was also in the room - she often built up a high blazing fire; she loved a big fire. He quickly brought in a metal bucket into which he shovelled the live coals. He moved away the furniture and rolled back the carpet; then with tools he hammered away to raise the tiled hearth to inspect under the floorboards. The ceiling in the shop was lined with asbestos, above that was the usual space before the flat's timber floorboards. Geoff saw to his horror a red glow travelling in lines along the joists up to five feet as the dust ignited. Fortunately flames had not yet developed. He hastily pulled away the side column of the fireplace surround to reveal burning, glowing debris. He continued to rip off the whole fire surround. Relieved, he and Jan mastered the fire with water without outside help.

The insurance company covered the cost of a new fireplace but not the decorating. The replacement buff coloured tiled fireplace was modern for the times incorporating ceramic tiles featuring birds.

BUYING A GROCERY BUSINESS IN CARDIFF

Still keen on owning and running his own business, Geoff bought a grocer's shop in Grange Town Cardiff. But the timing was wrong. The big food stores were starting to spring up. It is likely that the previous owner realised what was round the corner and got out in good time! Geoff soon found out that people were buying from the big stores at less than the wholesale price that he had to pay!

His customers grumbled even though he sold some regular items at a loss to attract custom.

The curse of the light fingers - He had other problems also for he discovered that a member of staff was sneaking cigarettes for herself and also selling goods and keeping the money proffered by the customer by omitting to record the transaction through the cash register. To compound the problem, change was given from the till. A cooperative member of staff noticed and reported this thieving but the awkward problem was in getting solid proof. He sacked the dishonest member of staff by making the excuse that they were overstaffed.

More trouble! He discovered that his wife was taking money from the till before it went through the books in the normal way! Frustration on frustration!

After about 4 years he sold up having made not a penny. He felt fortunate to escape bankruptcy.

The artful dodger - Geoff remembers an amusing incident involving a mouse!

Vermin can be a recurring problem in food shops. If you keep a cat you have to be careful that the cat, or dog, is not harmed by the war waged on the pests!

The current dog, Midgie, a small white silky curly-furred dog, started to take an excited interest in the bacon-slicing machine. Geoff investigated around and under the machine to discover a mouse hiding on the workbench, actually *under* the bacon-slicer!

The creature should have been swept on to the floor by the mechanism of the machine for when the slicing blade was moved - by hand of course! - a metal arm underneath, that was part of the action, would sweep across and back. He bent to see what happened to the mouse when he operated the machine, expecting it to be swept to the floor. He was amazed to watch the mouse duck every time the arm arced under the machine!

He found a long slim tool to dislodge the mouse and all the while the little dog was looking up in feverish excitement. Suddenly, to the astonishment of man and dog, the mouse jumped down using the *dog's nose* as a stepping-stone to reach the floor and scurry away before Midgie collected his wits! He must have felt grossly humiliated for in fact he was almost as good as a cat in the role of mouse catcher!

Beetle mania! - Geoff inherited an old large cool cabinet with the grocery shop. He decided to upgrade it and buy a new one. To his horror when he moved it he found a pile of straw and rubbish that turned out to be a nest of black beetles kept cosy by the warmth of the motor. They rushed out in all directions - dozens of the horrors! An anti infestation programme was duly launched with much vigour! It took some days to rid the old premises of the pests.

Whiskey the cat -Whiskey was a pretty black and white cat. He had white paws, a white chest and a white tipped tail. He was very affectionate, intelligent and a good mouser. The sound of pattering mice feet was once heard in the loft; Geoff sent up Whiskey who after a period of noisy mad scuttling appeared at the open hatch with two mouse-tails hanging from his mouth! Also on another occasion in the kitchen he managed a double catch. Whilst living in the first marital home in Newport, Whiskey's record of catches included: - a pigeon, a mole and a rat. All trophies would be deposited proudly on the doormat. Yuck!

At one time Whiskey shared the home with another pet - Bruno, a sheepdog cross. He used to love taking Bruno unawares; he would lay in wait hidden behind the gate and leap on Bruno when he appeared. Fortunately, Bruno was placid tempered.

Some years later when Midgie replaced Bruno, Whiskey tried the same shock tactics on Midgie, but he would growl and run away, neither would he enter into any fun-games. Whiskey would creep up and launch himself on Midgie when the latter was dozing in front of the coal fire - Midgie was not impressed!

THE FINANCE COMPANY

Geoff's task here was to make house visits to persuade people to settle their debts that had accrued from failing to make the regular higher purchase payments. Sometimes the debt was serious.

Geoff enjoyed the challenges that this job presented and there was much human interest to boot; but as in taxi driving this job brought him into contact with an unpleasant class of people who seem to have an essentially parasitic attitude to life The kind who seem to regard it a sport to withhold money rightly due to others, for as long as possible. He met with abusive aggression and even threats. He found that some bad payers were in genuine poverty, but certainly, not all those who practice a life-style of debt can be classed as genuinely poor.

The job paid quite well if one put in plenty of unsociable hours, but some confrontations were exceedingly unpleasant to the point of dangerous!

One of Geoff's tasks was to extract money from customers who owed for electrical goods including televisions. There was a 'save and view' scheme whereby the customer would be charged 'pay as you go' that was in excess of the real cost, the extra would be given back to the customer when the meter was emptied periodically. Also, televisions would be bought on a higher purchase arrangement. But some would fail to pay and appeared to have no concern about longstanding serious debt. Some fed buttons or pieces of round metal into the TV meters.

"I'm going to kill you!"

Geoff turned his head and got the shock of his life, only inches away, brandishing a kitchen knife in his hand, was an outraged youngster! -

Quite often it was Geoff's task to repossess televisions. One family was moving away so had to relinquish their rental TV. Before going into their living room to take the TV set Geoff had a word with the mother of the family who was working in the kitchen.

Two children were squatted on the floor, eyes riveted to the silver screen. With more efficiency than tact he walked up to the telly and unplugged it. He was about to move it when the younger of the two children, aged around 5years, in murderous rage, screamed.

Fortunately mother rushed in and rescued Geoff from a very scary incident if not a bloody fate!

"That'll teach you!" Geoff thought to himself as he cut the TV aerial with his pliers. He had made several visits to this particular house to repossess the TV and he never had a response at the door despite often telltale signs that they were at home. One day in frustration he severed the T V aerial. A few days later he learned that the old family had gone and a new family had moved in! - Oops!

Wanton damage -There were times when he had to repossess a nearly new T V too damaged and marked to be re-issued. Sometimes a set would be stained and sticky due to spillages of tea, booze or whatever, sometimes spills getting inside the set. Some almost-new TV's were only fit for the scrap heap!

Some salesmen were interested only in finding a new customer regardless of their integrity, in order to receive the commission due. The following story tells of the consequences of reckless, feckless, greedy, sales tactics

FRUSTRATION

Geoff went to one household that was in a disgusting filthy, smelly condition with the revolting odour of cat urine, and whatever! The woman of the house had a babe in arms! When Geoff became involved he found washers and metal discs in the TV meter. He advised the local shop Manager to give him the authority to repossess the set but a month later the address still appeared on his list for normal meter-emptying visits.

A month later he visited this customer...lo and behold! to his shocked dismay he discovered that a new set had been delivered - there was still no money to collect. No genuine coins had ever been put in the new set.

On the next visit the woman of the house, arms akimbo on the defensive, greeted him thus-

"It's out in the back-yard... smashed up!"-

Geoff could not believe what he was hearing. "What?"

"The fellar I live with came home drunk and he smashed it up in temper!" No apology.

Geoff was fuming at the salesman who irresponsibly placed the set there only to get his commission! When Geoff reported the matter back at the office they could scarcely believe it either; he was instructed to retrieve the damaged parts.

"But the TV set's in splinters!" -

"Well you'll have to get some for evidence."

Geoff refused "*You* go back to that stinking place, if you must!"- His resolve was set in stone! He did not return to that house of horror - nor did he lose his job.

Moving on - Geoff was one of the most successful employees at extracting owed money but the firm unrealistically increased the targets so he moved on. Also, there is an unrelenting strain in working with feckless people who exhibit no ethical code when it comes to money and live by a 'them and us' philosophy in their attitude to debt, viewing those to whom they owe money, with arrogance and aggression, regarding them as interfering nuisances.

THE SCHOOL OF LIFE CONTINUES

After working for the finance company Geoff became a food consultant promoting and selling freezers. He took to this job like a duck to water, again enjoying the challenge: sadly he came up against an even worse example of dishonest human beings - but that is another long story.

He then worked for a car-sales firm but when trade became brisk giving good commission for the sales-men the boss started to interfere and dealt with many of the sales himself! One colleague soon left in disgust, he was an ace salesman! Eventually he had his own business.

A little later Geoff also left especially when the boss started talking about a seven-day week. He was already working 10hours a day and more for six days a week with a half -day on Thursdays.

He worked for a time as Manager of a DIY store in Caerphilly S Wales. There were small wall pictures for sale. By chance he noticed three hidden in the staff cloakroom behind one staff member's coat; they were obviously to be smuggled out of the shop. He confronted the shop assistant, a youngish woman. She denied the accusation. Geoff stated the rule of buying through the manager at discount. He took no further action but a little later this woman in revenge wrote to the management accusing Geoff of making a pass at her in the stock room,

Geoff went through a very harrowing time during which he was called to head office to make a statement; he was under suspicion until another shop assistant decided to admit that she knew what this colleague was up to. The woman left but eventually wrote Geoff a letter of apology; this was truly an answer to prayer.

Conspiracy to rob - In this same job he thwarted the plans of a pair of thieves. A man and woman were working together. The man entered the shop and came to Geoff to ask him various questions about kitchen units. Shortly afterwards a woman came in and was browsing. As Geoff was talking to the man he needed to shift his position to keep an eye on her but the man seemed to move to block his vision and that made Geoff suspicious. But he did see the woman quickly slip bathroom scales into her shopper. She had nipped out and along the busy street before he caught up with her. Typically no member of staff was around. The man quickly left the opposite way. Geoff caught up and challenged her. She came back to the shop with him and he retrieved the stolen item but could not use the phone because it was in the downstairs office. Frustrated he had to let the woman go. He found that he needed to be very sharp eyed in the shop as thieves work in pairs.

Another act of dishonesty in this position was too much of a hassle for Geoff within a mere two-year period. The story goes as follows: -

Geoff took two weeks of holiday when a young assistant sales Manager was appointed from another branch; but he was taken for a ride by one of the usual sales staff, Gordon. Geoff and other staff had noticed that Gordon was always eager to handle money on the till. When Geoff was away this man industriously embezzled the firm in a big way with the cooperation of the van driver. Along with the normal orders they were loading other gear to sell themselves whenever they could. Also, purchases had not been through the till and on stock taking huge discrepancies were found.

Gordon in the space of two weeks had swindled the firm of the value, approximately, of one quarter of a normal month's takings.

Here is another mystery of the working of the human mind - that is, its tendency for failing to see the inconvenient obvious Even the most inept detective could have 'nailed' him! He left a 'paper chase' of clues scattered around. He was a pleasant guy, a family man, but he spent eighteen months in goal for his bungling thieving schemes.

DEATH BY DEGREES

When Geoff was the manager of a busy petrol and diesel filling station in Newport S Wales, he had many regular customers. One day he noticed one of the regulars, a man in his late forties, open the passenger door and push out a wheelchair that he opened whilst he remained in the car. It became apparent that he was without legs.

Geoff went up to him to offer help that he declined but he proffered his payment of £2 and then helped himself by wheelchair to the fuel. He returned to the offside of his car, shuffled in propelled by his hands, and hoisted in the wheelchair. Then he shuffled over into the driving seat. But the engine failed to start. He got out again using the same procedure, went round to front of the car - lifted the bonnet and started to fiddle with something. Again he declined Geoff's help.

"I know what the problem is," he declared confidently. Satisfied that he had done what was necessary he returned to the car and settled into the driving seat.

Geoff was now curious about his disability and asked him, "Have you been involved in an accident?"

"No." was the reply. He explained that he had suffered pain and circulatory trouble in one leg and eventually amputation was needed. He was a heavy smoker. The surgeon warned that if he went on smoking he would surely lose the other leg, or worse. He continued the fatal habit. As the surgeon had predicted - in due course he lost his other leg.

Geoff said, "What! Do you still smoke?"

"I'll never give up my fags!"

"All the best for the future!" called Geoff anxiously as the legless man drove away.

Some weeks later he learned from a colleague that the man had died.

CHAPTER FIVE

ROMANCE

GEOFF WAS TALL, SLIM AND upright in his teens. He was favoured with thick black wavy hair and full lips. He had/has hazel eyes graced by long lashes of which his sister was quite envious! He was shy, but a courteous manner and presentable dress appealed to the girls. Romance was the emphasis in those early relationships. Sex was not generally considered an option for most young couples in those days except sometimes when war service parted young couples and chances were taken.

Violet: Probably his first friendship with a girl was with Violet; she was bubbly and fun loving. She worked in the sweet shop through which the barber's customers had to walk. Geoff helped her organize the shelves and windows of the shop, which was owned, and run by the same couple as the Barber's shop. She was 18yrs old and senior to Geoff by four years but she took a shine to Geoff; he was not as smitten, as he was so much younger but they were good friends. He remembers once playfully putting his arms round her waist and she drew his arms closer to her.

In those war days shop windows were dressed with dummy products made of cardboard the colours of which often became faded in the sunlight making them sad and tacky looking! Sweet jars would be filled with empty wrappers because when sweets came in, the regular customers immediately snapped them up. Sweets were rationed but some products were off ration and she would save some for Geoff - a token of her affection! On one occasion she invited him to return to the shop after hours to pick up the goodies but he declined because of fear of being caught by the owners. Violet left to become a nurse and Geoff was surprised how he missed her.

For a while he went out with a girl who replaced her who was around his own age.

Wendy: The first girl he formally asked for a date was Wendy. She was of medium height and build with fair wavy hair and small neat features. She had a gentle disposition. They met when she was a general grocer's shop assistant. They were both in their mid teens. Geoff was regularly delivering goods to the shop, working for a food distributor. He drove, not a white van, but a horse and cart, a familiar sight on the roads in those days. The horse, Billie, was a lovely silver/grey. (There is more of Billie in the chapter 'Horses, Humans and Others')

Geoff was rather too shy to approach her directly so he gave a note to the manageress to pass on to Wendy.

"I like you very much and would like to have a date with you, how about it? Please let me know." The note said.

The next day Geoff visited the shop with heart in mouth but, it was her day off. - Typical!

On the next visit he met the manageress; on enquiring about the response to his note he was advised to see Wendy himself, his heart dropped! But Wendy soon appeared from the stores, smiling in demure fashion.

"Why didn't you approach me yourself?" she asked.

"Well, what's your answer?"

"Yes!" She said rather shyly; but there was a condition, that Geoff would pick her up at her home so that Mum and sister could eye him over! He complied with terms that included returning Wendy home by 9.30pm and he was passed as a suitable date!

Wendy was a steady girl friend for 4years 6months. She was faithful to him, writing regular letters during the 3.5years that Geoff was in the Army. In all that time they met up only once. Through all the time that Geoff was away she had visited his mother regularly on a weekly basis But in the Army doubts began in his heart and mind that Wendy was not the one he should marry.

The fact that he agreed to be a pen pal with Pat, a friend of one of his mate's girl friend back at home, indicated that he was not feeling committed to Wendy.

Pat: It was about a year before he was due out of the Army that he started writing to Pat. Their letters became quite long and became more humorous and witty than those with Wendy. He once wrote thirty-two pages of mirror writing - or backhand - Pat managed seven pages in reply! In fun, they wrote like this for a while! She said that she had to struggle with a mirror for some time to read his voluminous letters!

Photos were exchanged. Pat was attractive, with wavy brown hair a good figure and with an obviously lively intelligence so they agreed to meet in Birmingham where she lived, when he was demobbed.

Soon after being demobbed the two arranged to meet in a main Birmingham station. Geoff would be alighting from a particular train. Pat described the coat she would be wearing.

The day came ... Geoff was wearing his demob suit - the normal Army provision on being demobbed, not the most flattering outfit! He got off the train and looked around - when the crowd dispersed no one was left, or emerged from the shadows. He waited for half an hour, but still no Pat. He decided to hail a taxi and gave the driver Pat's address: the journey cost £2, a small fortune in those days.

The house was situated in an area of mostly terraced cottages. Pat's mother opened the door. Geoff explained himself. She knew nothing about the arranged meeting! Strange! Geoff felt uncomfortable but he was invited in and made welcome, fed, and invited to stay the night. This meant Pat sleeping in the bath - this was not an unusual arrangement in those days - the house had only two bedrooms. The next day he and Pat went into town for the morning. Though pleasant and friendly she remained aloof; an attempt to hold hands was shaken off. Before they were due to part he asked if she wanted them to meet again. Geoff expressed interest, she said that she would get in touch - as he expected, she never did!

On the homeward bound train, Geoff thought gloomily - what a miserable wasted effort that was. The only logical explanation for what had happened was that Pat had secretly viewed him at the station, did not care much for what she saw and like a coward departed. But she reckoned without Geoff's determined initiative! She must have been stunned when her Mum announced his arrival. Using a taxi, he probably arrived only a little while after she did herself. That is, if she had bothered to go in the first place! It was a rather ruthless way to deal with a young man just out of the Army.

Geoff left the Army matured, with a different outlook. Quite a normal development for young men following a spell in the Services.

Doubts about his relationship with Wendy crystallised when he resumed courting her after he came out of the army. It was with alarm that he realised that he must terminate their relationship as his feelings were not strong enough for marriage; she was still a lovely attractive girl with a sweet nature but he was aware of an unease in his heart.

They tried to resume their relationship on a friendly basis, but it was tense and unnatural. Perhaps Wendy was hoping for a change of heart. After a while Geoff had to back out; he could not continue the friendship. After deep pain and disillusionment, it rarely works.

On that last fateful night of meeting, whilst saying good night to her on her front door step he took a deep breath and said,

"I'm sorry Wendy, but I feel that I cannot continue, my feelings have changed, I don't think that we have a future together. I know that you will be dreadfully hurt... I hope that we can stay as friends."

At that she burst into tears and Geoff turned away feeling a dreadful heel. He trudged home with a heavy heart aware of how loyal she had been.

Wendy was deeply heart broken. The price of love is vulnerability and pain.

From that day his name was mud of the foulest kind in the Wendy household. Geoff's Mum also was upset because she had taken to the girl and naturally thought of her as a future daughter in law.

Mercifully, life moves on - *if* we let it.

More than 20years later Geoff bumped into Wendy in a shop. Life had moved on favourably for her. She looked well and spoke proudly of her two grandchildren.

Jan: Sometime later Geoff met another girl, Jan, she was blamed for the break up with Wendy, but this was quite untrue. It is strange how we feel happier to find a scapegoat to blame when things go wrong rather than accepting that life presents us all with twists and turns and changing fortunes.

Geoff's sister Joyce wanted to learn ballroom dancing and persuaded Geoff to be her partner. Up to then he had never been to a dance but he soon became very happily involved. He came to take it quite seriously, eventually to attend dances six evenings a week - it kept him fit! The dancing instructor Les, guessed that Geoff and a girl called Jan would make ideal partners, they did in fact find that they enjoyed a good rapport as a dancing duo and they started taking part in competitions They subsequently gained the bronze certificate in ballroom dancing.

Jan was a petite shapely girl with mid-brown nearly straight hair, which she usually bleached. She had a bright intelligence and quick sense of humour. She loved to be in company and would ably attract an audience with her repartee and wit. But she could be very sharply critical if things did not please her - in a restaurant for instance.

She could read rapidly, enjoyed educational books and was gifted with a photographic memory. After reading a book, if she was asked what was written on a specific page she could quote it. She worked on a comptometer (an old-time calculator) for most of her working life. Sadly she started suffering from severe bouts of asthma from the age of 17yrs. She valiantly tried to live life as normal ... but never gave up smoking.

Actually, when Geoff met Jan dancing she was courting a fellow, Richard, who was not interested in dancing. But after dancing with Geoff - once a week for a few weeks - he asked her to go on a date. At first she declined, but she considered the idea for about a month because she had been seeing Richard for three years. She finally decided to make the break and started courting Geoff.

For the second time Geoff played an integral part in the distress and disappointment of a family - this time it was Richard and his family..

Jan was about 18yrs old at the time - Geoff - 21yrs.

Helen: Geoff had been courting Jan for over a year when he met Helen, aged 18yrs.

He met her when he was taxiing hospital patients back home. Helen worked on the hospital switchboard. They struck up a friendship and there was obviously a mutual attraction.

Helen was a natural wavy blond - healthy and vital - a sporty girl - loved playing tennis. There was also an appealing impishness about her. She had a good voice and once went to a recording studio to record a song. She was an all round attractive girl with a robustness that was absent in Jan.

She enquired about Geoff's marital status of Dennis, a colleague in the taxi firm. Geoff discovered that Dennis, who was married with a young child, strongly fancied Helen and was jealous of the blossoming friendship between the girl and Geoff. One day Geoff asked Helen if she fancied Dennis. "No!" She said, "But anyway, he's married"

Later she told Geoff about a conversation that had taken place between herself and Dennis.

The ultimate test! - Dennis asked Helen this question about Geoff: -

"Do you like Geoff enough to use his toothbrush?"

What an intriguing and novel gauge of how to judge the level of mutual attraction and passion!!

Her reply was, "Yes!"...'Nuff said!

Occasionally one of Geoff's duties was to take a specimen from the hospital to a laboratory for analysis in Porthcawl, Glamorgan. It meant that Geoff was hanging around for two or three hours. One such trip started about 7pm. Geoff required an escort for which Helen volunteered!

Having deposited the specimen the two had time to wander along the promenade. It was dark by this time except for the normal street lighting.

"There was a gorgeous moon ... so romantic!" Geoff remembers.

They went back to the car and parked up in a parking spot overlooking the sea and moonlit sky. They kissed and cuddled. On the way back Helen snuggled into him. There were further such trips. There were times when Geoff escorted her home at 10pm after her pm shift. Before she ran to her front door they would linger for hours leaning against the Church wall at Christchurch (just on the borders of Newport) that was situated next door to her cottage home. A couple of times her Mum came out to remind her about getting up for work in the morning!

Jan was still in the picture but he knew it was decision time. Geoff was honest about his steady girl, he told Helen about her. But meeting Helen sent him spinning into a maelstrom of conflicting emotions. He had strong feelings for both .He questioned whether his feelings for Jan had been artificially fuelled by their mutual enjoyment of dancing.

~

A special bond is always formed between two people who share the same passion or work *together* towards a shared goal.

~

Decision time - He decided to tell Jan that he needed a month's break to test his feelings. He did not mention Helen. He explained his decision to Jan at the end of one evening - some minutes before her homeward bound bus came along. Reminiscent of Wendy Jan burst into tears at the bus stop and when the bus came she rushed up to the top deck hoping for some privacy in her grief.

Again Geoff felt dreadful and even worse than the time he had split with Wendy for on this occasion he had a niggling doubt whether he had acted wisely. Again, he received a lot of flack, this time from Jan's parents.

A very difficult decision faced him again. He now loved two women! The relationship with Jan had grown steadily based on a mutual enjoyment of ballroom dancing. It can be a romantic setting in which to form a relationship providing the most convivial atmosphere for fostering a romantic attachment - the attractive lighting, the pleasant music and the becoming dress of the dancers.

He painfully remembered walking out on Wendy and hated the thought of upsetting Jan; they had been going out steadily for over a year ... and yet ... there was a frisson between Geoff and Helen that was absent with Jan - Which feeling was the genuine one? Helen seemed to be brimming with fitness and vitality. Jan was petite, quick witted with a bright intelligence but seemed more fragile.

Helen was obviously weighing up Geoff as possible husband material when she tentatively asked the question one evening -

"Do you intend to stay a taxi driver?"

"Oh no, it was just to get a bit of money together, especially with the overtime and tips"

She went on - "My father would give you a position in his firm!"

His firm imported potatoes. Apparently her father had suggested this to her. Yes, Geoff would certainly consider this.

But the pull towards Jan was the stronger. Her face haunted him. He felt guilt ...and pity. After he split up with her on the Thursday, he phoned her the following Monday evening.

But the reunion was not exactly straightforward and spontaneous because Jan had lost confidence and was also influenced by her parents who were angry and they felt that it would be unwise to resume the relationship. However, after much hassle and heart searching on both sides they decided to give it another whirl.

...And now it was Helen's turn to be broken hearted! Yet another saddened family!

And so it goes on - the hopes and the crashes - the bonding and the breaking.

Betrayed

My thoughts and dreams I thought were sound.
So sudden were they dashed to ground.
My heart was full of joyful bliss,
But found the truth was only this:-
A hollow love- an empty hope.
In dark confusion round I grope.
I weep and cry 'til tears no more
My soul is shattered to the core.

But life moved on for Helen, she met someone new after a couple of years and married him.

Jan aged 23 and Geoff 26 married after a 3year courtship giving time to save up.

But a time of painful heart searching would come years later when Geoff forlornly wondered if he did indeed choose the right path at that significant crossroads in his life. If pity had been the strongest motive to resume his relationship with Jan it was a weak base. Perhaps a feeling of insecurity crept into Jan's feelings at this point that may account for future problems.

~

To sink or swim -Most of us are faced with a terribly difficult decision at some point in life. Sometimes it is a choice between the tug of the heart and the rational logic of the mind! If things go badly wrong with the course of action that we have chosen we can never know for sure if the alternative course would have been a success. There are too many imponderables. Wisdom can tell us that regrets will spoil what we have now and can ruin great possibilities of future satisfaction as yet unseen. Life will so often give us another chance - which may seem less desirable, but again, this view is based on unknown factors.

Sadly there are those who choose to masochistically wallow in their pain, becoming arid in soul-destroying self pity - thinking and acting as though no one else is capable of deep suffering, as though the level of their suffering were unique. Self-pity blinds one to new opportunities and shrivels the soul.

How we handle the mistakes that we make or the mistakes that others make affecting our destiny is the important issue in life. There is a spiritual perspective. We can choose a negative approach or a strong positive one. Whether we grow in maturity or shrivel in regret and bitterness depends on our decision.

The choice is ours!

~

CHAPTER SIX

A Form Of Death

Life progressed reasonably well for about eighteen years after his marriage to Jan. There were the usual ups and downs that are common to most people. Geoff had hoped to set up his own business and experienced two failed attempts but he shook off these setbacks in his normal buoyant 'bounce back' style.

Their accommodation had progressed to a comfortably roomy ex- farmhouse surrounded by farm fields with the sea about a half-mile away. There was a stream abutting their rear boundary. The land was flat but there was a high bank for protection. There was much wild life and bird life all around and footpaths in many directions. They felt that they had progressed to their dream house and would not wish for better. But unforeseen, soon it was all to disintegrate.

Health problems - Jan, at the age of eighteen, suddenly developed asthma - it was in the family. Asthma is when the bronchial tubes leading to the lungs go into spasm and cause breathing *out* to be a distressing problem. Jan would go blue for lack of oxygen. There were periodic trips to the hospital, the Royal Gwent, Newport, where she would be given emergency treatment in Casualty. This involved a large injection, using a big syringe. Often after an attack she would suffer a severe headache and would be so drained that she would sleep for 24 hours. As the years went by she was less responsive to the treatment. She tried valiantly to lead a normal life despite these episodes and was always fully employed - but she never stopped smoking! There was an anxiety about her health throughout their marriage

There was another medical problem - one day she developed severe abdominal pain. She was doubled up, screaming, on the verge of collapse when the ambulance came. But on the journey the pain suddenly went to the relief of them both.

When the Doctor saw Jan she said, "I feel a fraud! The pain seems to have settled down!" The doctor listened to her report and then examined her. He straightened up, looking grave.

"We must arrange for an operation quickly, you may have a cyst that has burst - it has relieved the pain but it could spread to cause poisoning of the system"

So the operation was done and it was as the Doctor suspected, an ovarian cyst had burst... and Jan lost an ovary, thus reducing her chances to conceive by half. The monthly cycle had always given her trouble.

Although children were longed for conception never happened.

Finances - They did not seem to be making headway financially despite the fact that they both worked and Geoff often worked long hours. Jan's habit of taking money out of the till when they had the grocery business was not helpful. Then Geoff discovered that she was routinely giving large gifts of money to her mother, a widow. This had been going on secretly for some time. This was a disappointing shock to Geoff - Jan also loved buying clothes.

The social scene - Jan complained that they, she and Geoff, rarely went out together, but their different work patterns worked against this, so he did not object that she made her own social arrangements. Jan loved company and could be very entertaining; she started going weekly to a private Club where a friend worked; but Geoff never fancied balancing on a bar stool whiling away the hours with small talk; in any case, a few of the jobs he had taken involved working late or doing evening work. So a different kind of leisure pattern was established for each of them.

Much later Geoff discovered that she had formed a succession of relationships of one sort or another with the men who used the Club.

Jan's sister on one occasion hinted that all was not well, she said to Geoff-

"Is it all right that Paul Hill goes to your house when you are in work?"

Paul was a mutual friend with whom Geoff had been out socially so he was not suspicious when Jan's sister made this remark.

The bombshell -The letter -

One morning Geoff was the first up for Jan was staying in bed that day suffering from a chill, so he checked the mail. One was addressed to Jan; he opened it as they did not have secrets from each other.

He was utterly stunned by what it revealed; it was from a man describing a very enjoyable date. To send a letter to their home address was so blatant that Geoff wondered if it was a way of breaking the news of what was going on. At the start of the letter were words that made his stomach contract -

"I enjoyed our time together - -"

It was from Paul Hill, their mutual friend - this cut like a knife. He bounded up the stairs to confront his wife.

"What's this all about? What have you been doing behind my back? Have you been having an affair?"

Jan waffled - "You shouldn't have opened my letter!"

"I didn't know that we had secrets. ... If that's the way you're going to carry on you had better pack your bags ... or I'll do it for you!"

Then Geoff had to depart for work. He was working as a food consultant for a freezer firm (freezers were the new 'everyone must have' rage at that time) he did many evening visits and such can be a strain on home and married life.

When he came back home from his day's work she was still in bed where she remained - mostly for the next two days. She had phoned in her place of work to take sick leave.

No one was speaking

On the second day he arrived home to find packed bags in the hall.

"Do you want me to go?" Asked Jan.

"It looks like you have decided to go ... I'm off back to work now, we need the money." Off he went to do some evening visits.

~

Communication falls down when we are deeply upset. Things are said in the hurt of the moment that are not meant but the one that hears them often acts upon them. Problems and hurts escalate when grim silence prevails. Funny how we can imagine wooing a lover back by screaming, accusing, bitter words, when there are welcoming, caressing arms waiting in the wings with murmured tender and romantic sentiments!

"Do not let the sun go down on your (wrath) anger." Says The Good Book, the Bible* because resentment and wild speculation grow out of all proportion when incubated and 'nourished' in the dark hours.

(* Ephesians 4:26)

~

Forsaken - Geoff phoned Jan at 8pm to inform her that he could be as late as 10pm. Sounding quite normal she lightly suggested that he do the late visit that he was reluctant about.

He returned home shortly after 9.30pm ...she was gone.

The fire was burning brightly in the grate casting a welcoming glow and some lights were turned on. But, the house had that ominous silence intensified by the knowledge that the human presence departed may never return.

Subsequently, discussing developments with mutual friends and his mother-in-law, he discovered, as do so many people in this situation, that he was the last one to know what several other people knew already - that Jan was spending time with Paul. No one had mentioned it to Geoff. He assumed that his doing evening work was a large factor in their marital disintegration.

A farmer/neighbour said that he had frequently seen a car parked outside of their home; it was Paul's.

The Mickey Finn - Geoff cast his mind back for clues that he had missed as to what was happening behind his back. Some months previously they had attended a wedding in Birmingham; at the reception in the hotel afterwards Geoff remembered having only two drinks but quite quickly felt ill with a thumping headache and he was sick.

He went to sit in the car for a while but felt no relief. Jan came looking for him at this point.

Together they decided that he needed to be driven to where they had planned to sleep over - at the bride's parents home. Geoff asked the bride's father to run him early to the latter's home to lay down; he was not too pleased to leave the wedding party thinking that Geoff had stupidly mixed his drinks. Jan said that he must have mixed his drinks - but no, this he never did.

Fortunately Geoff was fit to drive home with his wife the next day.

Thinking about this episode in retrospect he believed that he had been knocked out to get him out of the way, for a friend at the wedding said that he saw Jan and Paul Hill sitting on the bedroom stairs talking and laughing between the hours of 10pm to past midnight,

A Grim Drive to London - Before Jan departed she left a note of her future address in London W1 where letters could be sent, with no apology for the distress that she had caused. Her mother denied knowing where she was. The following day Geoff went to work and though he did not knock off until 7pm he had decided to rush up to London on the M4 after work and confront his wife. But he had no idea where in WI the address was located but desperation was the fuel in his tank!

Detective work - He found himself in the WI area of London - the time - past midnight. To seek help he stopped and asked a pedestrian, conveniently walking by. Uncannily, the address for which he looked was in the next street! The address seemed to be a flat over newsagents but being unsure he decided to doze the night away in the car. He was roused by a van turning up at the newsagents' at 4a.m. presumably with the day's papers. He went to enquire at the shop. He was shocked and felt painfully cheated to learn that in his hand he held an accommodation address! His emotional journey was for nothing. He drove back home deeply weary.

A FORM OF DEATH

In angry frustration Geoff went to his mother-in-law and finally extracted a clue about his wife's whereabouts. Despite a heated confrontation between the two the relationship was not broken for some weeks later when Geoff became homeless she offered him a home until he could be independent again.

The clue given by his mother-in-law about his wife concerned her new employment - it was near Manchester. She was working for a haulage firm called Turner and Newel. Geoff phoned Directory Inquiries and obtained the firm's head office number. Head office then gave him the number of the Manchester branch. Geoff asked for their personnel department. "She is off sick" he was told. He pleaded with them to divulge her address - said that his wife, a sick woman, had gone missing from home but she relied heavily on emergency medication. There was great reluctance to give personnel information but Geoff persuaded them and so he discovered her whereabouts and telephone number in Altrincham

A confrontation –As soon as was practical Geoff made yet another trip to save his marriage.

He found the address in Altrincham after making several inquiries.

It was evening and still light. He decided to hang around in case he got the chance to spot his wife or lover. He tried to creep stealthily up the drive to peer in a window but the gravel underfoot was noisy! He retreated and hid behind a tree. A man passing by thought that he was loitering with intent and challenged him! Geoff's rejoinder was hardly in terms of sweetness and light! - It certainly did nothing to calm the man's suspicions who hastened on but was obviously responsible for the appearance of a police car a little later! However at that moment Geoff was in a local phone box phoning the number that he had been given.

Geoff was in luck! Jan answered his call and she gasped audibly when she realised that she had been traced. Mercifully they managed some form of civility and he was invited in to discuss their future. Paul was not at home. But she did something amazing and quite preposterous! With obvious pleasure she actually showed him around the house (rented) even to leading Geoff into the double bedroom! How peculiar that Geoff submitted to this unjust humiliation!

After a long discussion Jan agreed to return home but needed a couple of days to sort things out. A specific train was decided upon for her to return to Newport to be met by Geoff .

So, Geoff returned home and anxiously awaited their reunion.

Daring to hope - He went to the station as planned - bought a platform ticket. The steam train came into view steadily entering the station and with a loud sigh of steam-powered brakes, came to a stop. Again with that peculiarly evocative powerful sound that steam locomotives make and with the awesome discharge of steam at pressure, the train moved off.

The steam cleared - the passengers dispersed - there was no Jan. He was miserably reminded of another time when he stood alone on a platform in Birmingham soon after being demobbed, to where he had made a futile journey to meet his pen-pal girl friend Pat. She never turned up!

There in that station, a meeting of hope with Jan became a meeting with misery. His spirit beaten and swamped in heavy rejection he returned home to his mum-in-law's house.

Jan was there! She was afraid to meet him in a public place for fear of an emotional scene. His heart thumped in trembling hope. He dared to wonder. - Another chance?

It was getting late; they talked into the night. Jan agreed to return home. Geoff had to go to work next day. He returned home after a long shift. Thankfully, mercifully, Jan was at home; she had spent the day industriously cleaning the house. The following day when Geoff arrived home from work, like a *deja vu* experience, for the second time he found a fire burning in an empty house and another fateful letter on the mantelshelf.

Jan had taken flight - again. Was this the final curtain?

Loss Compounded by More Loss! Catching up with personal business he discovered that the mortgage had not been paid for six weeks - simultaneously he found himself without a job because the so 'efficient' freezer firm he worked for turned out to be a small alliance of clever rogues. Geoff had worked several weeks on false promises of good commission - he received only two lots of commission despite winning many customers. He was now in debt with no income and as his status was 'self-employed' he was not eligible for dole! (Unemployment benefit) He was to be out of work for several weeks.

Life had suddenly and unexpectedly become grimly bleak; everything was disintegrating around him. He had no option but to break up his home at great financial loss and sell the lovely house and contents because he could neither afford to pay off the missed mortgage repayments nor continue the payments on his income alone. His furniture went to auction and some good pieces attracted very low prices. However, after some weeks he was in work again, strangely by the action of Jan who realised his dire predicament. Jan phoned Eddie, a man for whom Geoff previously worked, to explain what had transpired. Eddie responded and phoned Geoff to offer him his previous job. So again he was in work that he enjoyed - selling cars.

Not quite beaten - yet - Geoff does not lose without a fight. Some time later he made another bid to take back his wife although they would have had to live with her parents until they rebuilt their life together and found a new home.

He returned to Altrincham on a mid-week day. After much haggling and persuasion, Jan agreed to pack a bag and return; she admitted that she still loved Geoff but not as a wife.

Geoff optimistically believed that even at that stage they could work things out.

They stopped at Services on the M6 Motorway for food and drink but emotions became heated again. They continued their journey but soon she was crying and passionately declaring in between the sobs, that it was not going to work between them. The rowing reached boiling point. Geoff's temper snapped, he could not reconcile himself to what was happening; in a terrible rage he depressed the accelerator and threatened to crash the car, shouting wildly,

"I will kill both of us!"

She leaned over and managed to put her foot on the brake with effect. The car swerved but came to a standstill. He steered on to the hard shoulder - threw out her bag, leaned over and pushed her out of the car.

"You can walk back!"

Geoff moved off - she cried hysterically.

"Don't leave me here!"

She stood there on the hard shoulder frantically waving. She cut a pathetic, lone, petite figure in the darkness of the night

With a stab of conscience and flash of sanity he stopped and walked back for her - weeping and shaking she had to submit and continue the journey.

"He tried to kill me!" Jan yelled on arriving at her mother's home.

It was the end of the road. Obviously, there was no future for Geoff and Jan.

Numbed by the end of a marriage that he had not viewed as even ailing, Geoff conceded defeat.

DANGEROUS RAGE

In those days an encounter with an angry Geoff was a formidable experience best avoided!

Geoff was capable of exhibiting such simmering rage that one could believe that he was close to losing all control. Though not broad in physique he has always been strong with height on his side at five foot ten inches plus. Nevertheless he has always maintained that he would never strike a woman.

But the Geoff of those days has gone - that is, since the Transformation when God miraculously changed his heart - his emotions. He gets cross of course and may argue, but not with the seething, dangerous anger of former times. He marvels at the profound change within himself - not engineered by his own efforts. Truly it was a Divine Gift for which he is endlessly grateful. His life has been enriched beyond measure.

This change has been related in the chapters: - "The day when God showed up." and, "The Amazing Transformation." The heart change or *heart transplant*, as it has humorously been called, is possible for all who have put their faith in and sworn allegiance to, Christ Jesus. However, generally speaking, steps of Faith are usually subtler and are often part of a process rather than a powerfully significant step or revelation as happened with Geoff. Positive choice however produces positive results.

A CHAPTER IS ENDED

Again Geoff miserably contemplated his awful situation. The life that he had loved and trusted had suddenly collapsed in a miserable heap at his feet. In a short period of time he had lost his wife, her relatives, his job and his home. Only two years had elapsed since the death of his dear mother and after eighteen years of marriage there was not the comfort or compensation of children. His father still lived in Hertfordshire.

Every meaningful part of his life had dissolved; he felt totally bereaved of all that he held dear

A significant period of life of two decades had ended with nothing to show but a mere £372 in his pocket.

He experienced *a form of death.*

A less robust individual would have gone off the rails, but Geoff, somewhere deep in his soul, possessed faith and optimism for the future, allied to a stubborn belief that all was not lost. He was not tempted to stumble down the paths of self-destruction by way of alcohol, gambling, and womanising, nor even by the more acceptable form of help in taking prescription drugs; but he did get his job back although the work situation was unsatisfactory - that is why he left in the first place!

Some months after the final split, Geoff was driving past his mother-in-law's house when he noticed Paul's car - a grey Hillman Minx parked outside. He slowed down just at the precise time when Jan and Paul were being shown into the front bedroom by Jan's mother; Jan's elder sister was with them, he was able to see the scene quite clearly - another heart wrenching episode. He was so upset and angry that he scrambled out of his car, approached Paul's car, opened the bonnet and yanked an electric wire from the car's distributor. With the dubious satisfaction of revenge, he drove off!

He could not know that he had glimpsed Jan for the very last time...until he viewed her eighteen months later ... cold and lifeless in a funeral Chapel of rest in Newport!

The long-term asthma had taken its toll. What turmoil of mixed feelings Geoff experienced that day.

We had not known each other long but I accompanied Geoff on this emotional visit - both thoughtful and in awe at this latest development.

A BRAND NEW CHAPTER OPENS

Geoff rented a flat for a while which proved draughty and unfriendly. His sister Joyce and husband suggested that he should buy a caravan and site it on their smallholding, which he did for several months, but the un-insulated van was very cold and wet with condensation. Moreover, this arrangement spawned its friction and problems.

But not many months passed before he met his new wife to be - Dorothy (me!) It was basically love at first sight He proposed on our second date and I accepted - a rash decision according to my mother at the time! In two weeks we were officially engaged to be married.

So big changes were in the pipeline of Destiny, or God's Hand - whatever! - A new start - new love - new home - new job - and though there were no children - a new future and new Hope. And some years ahead, a new and vibrant Faith.

Geoff stopped smoking. Alcohol had never been an attraction. He once got drunk and badly ill after drinking too much whiskey, he meticulously avoided this scenario for the rest of his life!

It was a new start for me as I had also suffered a long haul of physical pain following a back and hip injury at work. There was also a string of heartaches and dashed hopes, all together triggering periods of depression. It was time to draw a curtain over past struggles.

~

Realism Replaces Unobtainable Romantic Fantasy and Idealism

There are grim periods in life when one has to find a way through deep agonising loss, disappointment and betrayal. Disillusionment threatens future contentment, but on the other hand it can birth a more realistic outlook and greater maturity of character bringing a keener appreciation of the simpler enjoyments. Greater tolerance can result, of situations, and yes, of people, that fail our expectations…as indeed we have failed others! It is the human condition!

When things of the senses let us down or fail to deliver - our thoughts and aspirations may turn to spiritual and creative things and a higher level of life and consciousness is discovered!

A Recipe for Success in a Brand New beginning in Mid-life -

Our new life together worked because we both drew a line under our past, which we did not muse on or mope over. Except for lessons learned we stamped the past '*episode finished*'. We did not allow past sad experiences, or the personalities that were involved, to be a focus of conversation for many years. The past now seems to be like a previous incarnation! (Not a belief of ours by the way!) Both of us brought the minimum amount of goods and chattel from the past into our new life together so there was nothing to argue, or sentimentally drool, over!

~

Banishing Regrets

The things we think that could have been,
Fine chances that we cast aside,
May not be what our dreams have seen,
May not have lingered by our side.
Surfeit with wealth or wanting a dime, all that is real is present time,
The yesterdays away have flown, tides of the future, yet unknown.

Ghosts of the past stir up our fears –
The former things we must forget
Why waste our strength in pain of tears?
And curse tomorrow with regret.
Imagination weaves romance of happiness we missed - by chance.
Brings anguish from the might-have-been. But, things are rarely how they seem.

"If only!" sighs make vain our prayer –
The thing we missed –what is our due,
And they become a deadly snare,
So oft remote from what is true,
Humans do err, we can be blind, but Grace will sweep us like a flood
When through humility we find - that God is real and He is good,

The time in life we lose our way
To heap distress upon our mind
Is time to find the Saviour's Way
Who speaks to us that God is kind.
If we, our days place in His hand, sufficient for today, our store,
Our inner self will rise and stand, in Winter's Day we need not more

So in the sad times of our years
When grieving sore that we've lost out,
When anger mingles with our tears
And we are tossed by mocking doubt
A balm may sooth the soul in pain to be transformed by Heavenly Light! -
And rise above this mortal plane, to walk by faith and not by sight!

CHAPTER SEVEN

THE "STRANGE OTHER" WORLD

EVERYONE MUST ENCOUNTER INEXPLICABLE OR unusual events. Some have seen angels. Geoff has had his fair share of irrational experiences!

In the early days of his first marriage Geoff kept a succession of pets. He has a repertoire of pet stories. Sometimes the behaviour and movements of animals are guided by an instinct or gleaned knowledge by some unseen sense not usually accessible to humans.

Here are a few pet anecdotes: -

A TALE OF THE HOMING PUSSYCAT

For a time Geoff was on the police team of a large firm. On one occasion, 15mins before his night shift was due to end at 5.30am, a pretty black and white kitten walked through the main gate and into the gate security office. It seemed in no mood to leave and as there were no dwellings nearby Geoff presumed that it was lost. He tucked it in his jacket and cycled over 1.5mls home. Whiskey, as he was duly named, settled in well for many months ... and grew.

Then Whiskey disappeared. Five months went by.

One morning, Geoff had cycled just a few yards homewards from work when a short distance away he saw a cat looking just like whiskey, only thinner, chasing another cat. Geoff called out "Whiskey!" He immediately responded and with an erect tail - denoting pleasure. He let himself be tucked into Geoff's jacket, again - purring. Back home he settled down as though nothing had happened.

The route between Geoff's home and work twisted and turned and it was mainly built up. A quicker route would have been along the railway track that ran at the bottom of the long garden. Was the cat guided this way by instinct? - An unsolved mystery. (Whiskey was over 14 years old when he died)

GEOFF ONCE HAD DOG CALLED BRUNO

He was like a small Labrador cum sheep dog with tan coloured medium length fur; curiously, one eye was blue, the other - brown.

Geoff's first wife's sister used to visit with her two young children and Bruno loved them. Naturally they would also visit the children's grandparents who lived beyond the railway line, pond and a further two streets away -diagonally placed. Remarkably, the children would have scarcely settled at the home of their grandparents when who would arrive in the garden but Bruno! The only possible route for Bruno would be over a mile through streets, under a low bridge and across roads. He had done this walk with Geoff but the vexed question was - how did he know that the children had arrived? Perhaps sensitive hearing was the key, but to humans it seemed an incredible feat! He must have remembered the route!

Another Bruno tale -

Geoff was sales Manager at a car show room that from home was a distance of two miles - of streets and roads, plus river bridge. The dog had never been to Geoff's place of work and Geoff always went by car so could not have left his scent, but one day Bruno simply turned up at the car show room! But Geoff was not there being away on an errand for the boss.

The dog sniffed around and then wandered off only minutes before Geoff returned when he went off immediately to look for him.

Going down a straight road Geoff heard a squeal of breaks and the yelping of a dog; his heart somersaulted. He stepped out of the car and there was his dog hobbling towards him on 3 legs. One front leg was bizarrely and loosely dangling, it was broken in two, and there was blood around his face and ear. The car was damaged also, which gave rise to an angry tirade from its owner! Never mind the poor wounded dog! - But he survived.

More inexplicable events: -

THE ACCIDENT THAT WAS NOT

Geoff was called up at the age of 18yrs, as was the custom then. He was stationed for Army training at Catterick N Yorkshire.

He was driving an army Bedford 3 ton truck through the lanes on a dark autumn evening with a Senior man. He was approaching a narrow single track bridge when the lights of a motor bike appeared - coming straight at him - - he anchored on and instinctively closed his eyes for a second, bracing himself for the inevitable sickening crash - on the bridge. . .It never came . . .dead silence...

He got out and shining a torch inspected all around and down the banks... he could find no sign of the motorbike or the rider.

Chatting later in a local village pub he was told that this bridge was haunted, there *had been* a fatal motorbike accident!

THE CAR THAT SHOULD HAVE BROKEN DOWN

This strange inexplicable situation occurred when Geoff was in the motorcar retail trade, at a period when he was in partnership with two other men. He would usually go up to London with a group of like-minded colleagues to attend the annual Motor-show. There were four of them on this particular occasion. It was around 1958.

They travelled from Newport, S Wales in a Vauxhall Wyvern, the Company car that had been on temporary loan for some weeks to Geoff for his personal use and running around for the firm. Geoff naturally was the driver for this trip.

The journey to London went off smoothly. The men enjoyed the show and were liberally plied with drinks, their hosts being under the impression that the four men were new-car distributors, and not sellers of used bangers!

They stayed overnight together in a four-bed room in a small hotel.

They were somewhat boisterous and merry into the small hours, tucking into a cooked chicken!

The occupant in the next room must have complained because a call came asking them to be quiet. A little later they received another call through the intercom from the same source.

The voice said, "Have things quietened down now? Is everything all right?"

Geoff answered the call, and stifling his spontaneous guffaw, sedately replied,

"Yes, it's all gone quiet now, thank you very much!""

The porter had buzzed the wrong room! This error was not very conducive to achieving the desired peace! However, a measure of dignity was restored in the group!

In the morning they returned to the show and set off back home around midnight. The journey was without incident. After dropping off his friends at their respective homes Geoff returned to his flat above the car showroom, parking the car on the forecourt.

The next day it was necessary to move the car as it was in the way, but it failed to start. Geoff who had basic mechanical knowledge (for the cars of that era) could not find the fault so he called in Dave the firm's mechanic. Diagnosing the fault as electrical he examined the appropriate parts. He removed the HT lead to check it.

All four heads of the men on the previous day's trip were clustered, bent over the bonnet, curious about the car's failure.

The mechanic loosened the coil lead and examined it in his hand. He checked each end and puzzlement registered on his face. He slit open the length of it with a knife - he stood up with a stupefied expression!

"I just can't believe it!" he exclaimed, shaking his head in disbelief, "I can't find *any wire* in the sheath of this rubber cable!"

There was no evidence of the presence of any wire - no burnt remains - no scorching or any other abnormality! He replaced this lead with a new length and the car started immediately giving no further trouble.

Electricity cannot travel along a rubber wire - rubber in fact being an ideal insulator, *not* conductor! The men debated the mystery from every angle but came up with no explanation whatsoever. The mystery remains to this day.

If there was no physical explanation to this seemingly miraculous event, was there in fact a spiritual one? Had the *other world within this world impinged* on the events of the previous day? For what purpose? Perhaps there was imminent danger on their long drive home from London and had they been stranded in a remote place in the dead of night they may have been exposed to some unknown serious danger. It does not explain why some people seem to be in the wrong place at the wrong time and suffer death or serious accident as a consequence.

The event poses another vexed question - The car was 10yrs old, at what point was this freak HT lead put in the car? ...

Nevertheless, thankfully, by good fortune or Providential Blessing, the car, most conveniently and graciously, whilst standing quietly on the forecourt, chose to expire!

N.B. The 1ft (30cm) HT (high-tension) lead connected the Coil to the Distributor to carry the electric current to the plugs to create sparks.

ANGELIC INTERVENTION

Many people testify to miraculous escapes from death when they have trusted in a loving involved God. Geoff has had enough near misses with death to believe that he has been the recipient of angelic intervention on his behalf on several occasions. He believes that an instinctive deep belief in a caring Providence is the key to this protection, a belief that was birthed in him when as a young child he was overwhelmed by the wonder of Nature. (See the chapter - An Awakening)

DRIVING THROUGH THE FLOOD

Geoff remembers another occasion when he was coming home late evening from London, it was very dark and there had been flooding rainstorms; he was driving a 1938 Austin 10. It was in the '50s.

Suddenly in the darkness and through the rain, a scattering of red lights became visible. They were the rear lights of stranded cars caught in a flooded area of the road. Geoff was in the water before he realized it; he quickly selected bottom gear. Steadily and slowly he manoeuvred around the stranded cars. The water entered the car almost covering his feet but he came through the flood. The engine spluttered and steamed but the car kept on moving. It eventually dried out and he arrived home safely. Again he felt very fortunate.

A PICTURE HOUSE TALE

Going back to the days of his youth - Geoff used to sneak into the cinema by the exit door when the people were coming out. There was the time when he smuggled in his pet dog; it was a kind of miniature "Lassie" dog named 'Lady' with long dark auburn fur and a fringed curly tail. She settled quietly on his knee. A woman came to sit by him with a friend, addressing her friend she exclaimed,

"Oh look! He's got a dog on his lap...but isn't she quiet!" He thought that his secret was out plus the fact that he had sneaked in, but nothing further happened, much to his relief.

But sometimes the films were of the extremely scary kind and gave him nightmares. He had a period of sleep walking, which he suspects may have been triggered by illegally watching horror films. He became very scared of the dark and Mum started the practice of placing a lighted oil lamp by his bed.

One night he awoke screaming in terror, the lamp was out, Mum rushed in and found him half way down the bed with his legs sticking out of the bedroom window! This was possible with the sash window. Fortunately those episodes ceased.

A GHOSTLY ENCOUNTER

Around that time, living in Newport, he and four other boys were exploring a large neglected house. A friend and family were living in one end of it - which was tidy. They were exploring the cellar region of the house that was reputed to be haunted. The cellar had rooms with iron barred gates instead of doors as though it had been a jail at one time.

As they were gingerly exploring the basement one evening, a figure in a white coat like that of a hospital doctor, rushed passed them and up the steps. The lads followed and saw him run down and along the riverbank, and vanish; this would scarcely have been possible because of the slope and the mud, which confirmed to them that they had seen a ghost. They all saw this apparition.

Did they have a glimpse of that *world within a world,* that elusive dimension? . People who have never seen a ghost do not believe in them, especially in our rational British culture but those who see one change their minds! *Seeing is believing* as we say.

There are people coming to these isles who are very much aware of that *world within this world,* they have much to teach us.

Some individuals have been terrified and psychologically harmed by the dark side; but others have been uplifted and liberated by the light side of this *world within the world*

THE PHANTOM OF THE HOSPITAL

I too have seen a ghost. I saw an elderly soldier in what was called 'hospital blue'. It was a darkish blue serge battle-dress style tunic with a kind of blouson top and fitted waistband. It was worn in hospital by recovering injured-in-war soldiers. I saw 'my' apparition as a student nurse on night duty in Pinderfield's Hospital, Wakefield. Chatting to a senior nurse some days later, I learned that I had seen the known hospital's ghost - a man from the First World War who had hung himself in a single room.

I thought at the time that I had seen a convalescing patient who had dressed and taken a little walk because he could not sleep. There was nothing spectral about his appearance. I remember clearly his face, silver grey hair and balding head.

~

There is no logical explanation why one should see a ghost, and what is 'it' anyway? No one has a truly convincing, *solid,* (pardon the pun!) reason for the possibility of such an encounter; there are theories. But! Normal sane people genuinely report them.

Belief in God is a parallel situation. To try to reason a way into belief by definite scientific proof to satisfy logic yields no definite conclusion. But for one who has had an experience of God, or by faith has been wonderfully changed on the inside, or has developed a vital daily relationship with God in Christ - the experience is glorious reality, scientific proof becomes unnecessary, irrelevant.

There are happenings in this life that seem to defy logical explanation. They run counter to our knowledge of the laws of the universe. When these strange things are recounted to friends one is accused of being overtired or jumpy (if it is a ghost) Or suffering from wishful thinking and overdrive in the imagination, (if it is a religious experience)! -Those are the kindly descriptions!

But the scepticism or hilarity of friends or foe changes nothing of the experience for the one who has actually lived it.

Similarly, down the years, Christians have faced horrendous deaths because they would not deny what for them had become the most real and precious reality of their lives, even worth suffering a tortured death.

~

A MIRACLE HEALING IN NORTH WALES

Coming to more recent times - in 1995 a meeting occurred with strangers with unexpected and beautiful consequences.

Geoff and I lived for nearly six years in a chalet bungalow in a small hamlet in Gwynedd North Wales between Caernarfon and the village of Llandwrog. In 1992 we moved to St. Martins north Shropshire to be near the canal system for we had owned a narrow boat (wrongly called a 'barge' by many) for some years and wished to be nearer the waterways.

It was during our time in St Martins that Geoff had a spectacular encounter with God (see the chapter 'When God showed up') This event led us into meeting a small group of Christians who lived out a strong faith and relationship with God in Jesus Christ his Son, with a belief in Divine/Faith healing using the Name (meaning the authority) of Jesus Christ.

Whilst living in our new location we rented out the chalet in N Wales for a time and then put it up for sale. We arranged to make a trip to see prospective buyers and with us to share a pleasant trip, we took Gladys a new Christian friend. It was a lovely summer's day.

The couple that came to view the chalet was in late middle age. It became obvious that they were under stress. She had a sickly pallid grey appearance, her face etched with stress lines. He looked dispirited and was probably unwell also. Naturally the conversation soon came round to why they were moving.

~

There are two basic reasons why people move. A happy reason is to improve their life style in one or more ways - a better job, a better school, to move nearer to loved ones, for a larger house to accommodate a growing family, a marital home for a new couple, the first home for a single person or to a better locality. When the reasons are positive there is an excitement, an eager attitude, and if the property is promising, immediately they mentally start moving in deciding where their furniture fits, where the garden shed will go, will the car fit the garage - and so on.

The second basic reason for moving is due to some form of reduced circumstances and a prospective buyer comes in a subdued spirit, even on the edge of breaking down emotionally, as a better, fuller life has come to an end and the vision of the future lacks lustre, or worse, looks dismal and joyless. To lose a good job with its comfortable home and life-style is another sad and unwanted obligation to move. Some take the necessary move due to old age with patient and pragmatic resignation even to feeling a sense of relief that a smaller dwelling will mean less work and responsibility. But the need to move because of worsening disability or terminal illness is a joyless affair requiring realism and courage. The future looks like a dark characterless page. It looms threateningly as a great test of patience or even endurance, laced with pain, physical or emotional.

~

The couple that came to look at our chalet were certainly of the second group, but they did not grumble or complain looking for sympathy as some people would but were being bravely practical.

They lived in a large house in the Midlands and they were looking for a small place to suit the husband because she had little time left being in the final stages of cancer. She was making frequent hospital visits; a phial of morphine had been implanted under the skin so that she could release a dose when the pain increased. A valve opened when the phial was pressed to administer the drug for pain. I believe that it was positioned in the chest area. Her husband naturally looked gloomy and strained and had in fact suffered a heart attack with the anxiety and stress.

We expressed our concern and I asked if they would appreciate prayer, stating our belief in the power of prayer; she unexpectedly fell into my arms with gratitude and eagerly accepted the chance of prayer but she did not attend any religious organisation. I seated her in a chair; her husband sat on the settee nearby. I prayed quite briefly asking the Lord for Healing but being aware that healing can come in the form of deep peace and calm acceptance of whatever is to come. Geoff also prayed, briefly. My friend Gladys prayed in a special prayer language that some Christians have received from God. Though never being in a leadership position or place of authority she spoke in a strong voice of command, which was simply not typical of her. Geoff and I knew that it was God's Spirit that was giving her special prayer force. See 'Note' at the end of this account.

The husband also was happy to be prayed for. After looking around they went home.

Some months went by and we thought no more about the incident, the couple had not phoned back so obviously the chalet did not suit their needs, as we had guessed.

Then we received the unintelligible end of a message on our answer phone; the voice was that of an unidentifiable woman. A little later she phoned us again when we were in to take the call. She was the woman for whom we had prayed in N Wales

What she said was quite unexpected and wonderful. She and her husband had been completely healed of their illnesses. I was so taken aback that I failed to take her number or ask for the details of their healing. She thanked me profusely but I explained that it was

God's Love and Power that had been at work. Perhaps all of the five of us had pooled our faith in strength together to bring it about.

I would like to record that this was the start of many such miracles but though there have been many answers to prayer with healing or improved health, this was the one most dramatic healing with which we have been involved.

There are clues and many theories but no clear-cut answers to the mysteries of spiritual or Divine healing and conversely, of non-healings. Harbouring destructive emotions of anger, resentment and unforgiveness have proved to hinder healing in *some* cases.

Note

Jesus of Nazareth when teaching his disciples on the subject of faith and prayer taught them to be authoritative, as a General would command his troops. Jesus, as was his style, used picture language in teaching spiritual truths.

In the Holy Bible in St Mark's Gospel chapter 11 verse 23 he taught -

"I tell you the truth, if anyone says to this mountain, 'Go throw yourself into the sea' and does not doubt in his heart but believes that what he says will happen, it will be done for him."

He used the word 'mountain' meaning 'obstacle' or 'sickness'. Also 'the sea' representing destruction. The implication is that a weak prayer will result in a weak result or no change at all.

Gladys in fact was commanding the sickness to go as though it were a nasty pest! This may seem strange and illogical but it was the extremely effective style that Jesus used. We can look at the time when Jesus brought Lazarus back to life, a man dead for more than three days and was already 'stinking'! The gospel of Mark records -'Jesus called in a loud voice, "Lazarus, come out!" The dead man came out!

A PREMONITION OF DEATH

Maurice the husband of my sister Mary (died 1988) was in a Huddersfield hospital during his short terminal illness in 1996 aged 84years; he had suffered a severe stroke.

We had stayed in his home for a while, visiting him and minding his affairs. But we had to return home. The hospital was about 100miles from where we lived at the time.

It was Friday evening at around 6.30pm, just a few days after coming home - Geoff and I were relaxing when Geoff suddenly sat up wide-eyed and alert; he turned to me.

"Dot, ring the hospital ...do it now!" There was an urgent note of command in his voice. He had received what is commonly called a premonition.

I phoned the hospital caring for Maurice and was transferred easily through to the ward where we had visited him only around three days previously. When I asked after Maurice the nurse in charge who answered the phone paused and appeared flustered:

"Er ...this is difficult for me...er! ... But naturally I have to tell you ...Your relative, Maurice ... has just passed away! I've just come from the side-room where we moved him ...the end was very peaceful but…er … it was my duty to tell a senior Nurse first of all ...but you have just rung ...!"

I explained that Geoff had just received a 'knowing' that Maurice had passed away.

The nurse was quiet, transparently stunned.

We returned to the hospital a couple of days later and were given the opportunity to view Maurice in the hospital Chapel; the porter discreetly left us for a few minutes.

There was a Gideon Bible on the table. Geoff picked it up and idly opened it. It opened in the middle pages of the book at Psalm 4. He read it out loud, but the last verse spoke with great clarity and comfort to both our hearts:

"In peace I will both lie down and sleep; for thou alone, O Lord, makes me dwell in safety" Psalm 4 verse 8.

It was as though Maurice himself was speaking those words.

I knew without a doubt that I was not seeing death but a state that Jesus Christ sometimes referred to as 'sleeping'. I *'knew'* that I would meet Maurice again some day!

When for a glimmer of light I so desperately grope,
Thou Lord of Grace and Love speaks quiet words of hope.
I'll cry to you with my trembling breath;

Thus I rise in strength in the face of death.
By faith within,
Death hath no sting.

Geoff touched Maurice on the forehead; he was ice cold for being kept in the Mortuary fridge.

"I wish I had not done that!" Said Geoff - he shuddered "It is better to remember loved ones alive, not like a block of ice - it is horrible! It's not really like that - he is changed, not dead." - These sentiments on Maurice's *real* state, three days later, would be wonderfully confirmed! Praise God!

~

Ghostly experiences often frighten ... Are they glimpses into the sad and troubled sphere of the dark side of the realm of spirit - the *plane of the lost* in the *other world*?

~

The next story, again concerning Maurice, seems to tell of a similar event to the phantom appearance of the soldier patient in hospital but yet is totally different in essence. Geoff experienced this encounter as *a vision,* a heavenly blessing, a glimpse into that beautiful *other world* sphere, it features an *appearing* that was designed to bless and comfort. An answer to prayer in fact!

"I'M ON MY WAY!"

My younger sister Muriel and I were executors of our brother-in-law's affairs. My sister had just had a hospital operation herself so Geoff and I made a start on the usual tasks.

On this sunny afternoon, Monday May 13th 1996 three days following Maurice's death, I was writing the usual letters on the dining room table overlooking the rear garden. Geoff was with me to help when in this setting something wonderful happened...

Maurice had lived alone for six years, for tragically, my sister Mary aged 61years had died of cancer - ironically she was 13years his junior - she was the third wife that he had lost through illness. There were no children. He had no siblings being an only one. Maurice felt this absence of family quite deeply ... naturally.

Before the loss of Mary, like so many, he had been a person with a quiet unspoken faith; a faithful worshipper and worker at the local Methodist Church ... until the strokes started. He lost much of his mental powers and memory in the last few months of his life, and sadly even lost the memories of Mary, whom he dearly loved. The strokes caused mental confusion - at one point he thought there was a family of squatters living upstairs in his home.

When Mary died, we wondered uneasily if his faith was firm enough to survive this terrible loss of a third wife who spent the last stricken days in a hospice...

I prayed much, with tears, for him.

Back to the dining room: I was writing the letters with a lump in my throat that had distressed me all day as I was selecting what clothes and things could go to the charity shops and which had to be dumped... distressing stuff!

I was busy with the pen, head bent forward when at my right I heard Geoff sob. I looked up. What he had to relate caused us both to weep, but this time, not in sorrow ... BUT in JOY, and the lump in my throat vanished!

Geoff recalls that what he saw was as clear as day-

"I saw Maurice standing beside me, in his light grey suit with collar and tie as normal. He had a gabardine raincoat over his arm, just as though departing on a special trip; he appeared young and vibrant.

"He looked at me and with an upward gesture of his arm said, 'everything is all right, and I'm on my way!' I sensed him move out of the room through the window and away towards the hills."

Our Heavenly Father had blessed us with such a precious gift! - A glimpse into that *world within a world*! What an incredible difference it made to our whole outlook on our loss and grief. It reinforced our belief that by Grace - made real by Faith in that Grace, we look forward to a wonderful new life one day!

And *we shall* meet Maurice again. That's for definite!

~

Listening to others and reading about the *otherworld* experiences of many people has taught us that lovely supernatural events cannot and *must not* be commanded, they are essentially spontaneous.

If we hanker after such events and try to make them happen whether in a religious setting or simply in someone's home, we may in fact invite some very undesirable, frightening or deceptive supernatural manifestations. There are energies around us that are not for playing or experimenting with - kind of wild psychic electricity, in a manner of speaking! What sane person would dabble carelessly with and in ignorance of electricity?

Many search for supernatural experiences but in fact they are expressing a misunderstood hunger and longing to find their lost relationship with the Creator God from whom all of us have become distanced - alienated. But God designed us to be his children, to be in intimate relationship with him as our Father and to enjoy a glorious non-ending life, a life that is beyond our imagination to visualise in our present physical state.

Wonderfully, Jesus is currently busy repairing this breach between human kind and God in the lives of very many people all over the world! But one day, as promised, he will come again to earth to be revealed to all as Divine King to complete his beautiful healing and repairing work!

The far, or could it be near? future is looking Good!

~

Very strange but Natural - Two Stories

A CAR SUSPENDED IN AIR!

On a recent holiday in mid Wales Geoff and I enjoyed a recommended scenic car drive through some of the largest tracts of wild, moor, mountain and lake areas in the Province.

We set off from Tregaron situated S East of Aberystwyth, the road climbing and bending through the varied contours of forest plantings and sheep dotted moor land, then curling around the large Llyn (lake) Brianne to descend into and through Rhandirmwyn

It was a blustery, showery, chilly week in March so the traffic was sparse. We expected no human interest of any note… how wrong we were!

We had just started the long twisting descent from the higher altitudes when we saw an amazing sight! We were travelling the typical 'shelf ' road that you find in mountainous regions. It was the kind of road that has been cut out of sheer mountain/hillside; the land was rising steeply on our left with a precipitous sheer drop to the right and just enough room for opposite flows of cars.

We had come round a gentle bend when on the right we saw a black Ford 'Focus' car, about 13years old, whose car bonnet was tilting downwards well over the edge, at a crazy 45degree angle, seemingly in the act of plunging into the lightly wooded deep chasm below.

Shocked, all sorts of thoughts and guesses rushed into our minds as we saw at a glance that if there were anyone in the car it would have been highly dangerous for them to step out or for anyone to touch the car from the outside.

We scrambled out of our car to inspect the scene. It was difficult to see into the car properly because of the angle but we could see children's items on the floor behind the two front seats. Thank God, no one seemed to be in the front or back.

Looking at the car, two thirds of it was actually hanging in space, but angled from the edge as well as pointing downwards at an angle. It had been transfixed in space! Why did it not continue its plunge of over 150 feet?

Then we saw that a finger of rock protruded out at an angle from a little below the surface of the road. The end of the finger of rock was jammed between the front of the engine and the base of the radiator, between the front wheels. Because of the dipped angle of the car the back wheels were elevated and the car's underside exposed! All the driver's side was completely out of reach.

What we saw did not make sense, we hoped that the owner had left the car before it had moved from its tiny patch at the edge of the road, but that meant it had been very poorly parked for the driver had left the car with the wheels turned outwards towards the edge and inches from the sheer drop. The road was not dangerously steep at this point. We deliberated on several possibilities. We even wondered if it had been a badly managed false accident that misfired to claim insurance.

To our great annoyance we had not brought a camera to capture the remarkable image nor could we use our mobile phone as they do not work in these remote regions. We went on our downward way intending to give the alert when we reached civilisation! It was about 3.30pm.

Approaching Rhandirmwyn we came to a young man hiking wearing a rucksack. Yes! He was the hapless victim, but unhurt and curiously phlegmatic about his predicament We picked him up and he was happy to be dropped off later near a pub. He was on a bird-watching day trip from Northampton, quite a distance for the shorter day of early Spring season. He explained that he had to leave his car in a hurry to answer the call of nature then returned to find his car hanging over the precipice! We shuddered to imagine retrieving a rucksack from the precarious car!

On our way back to our holiday cottage we discussed this incident at length. The man was suitably insured but though the car seemed little damaged at this stage we could not imagine a successful rescue mission as the road was narrow for the manoeuvres of a lifting crane. But how would one fix the lifting straps? Rescue men would need to be half suspended!

Afterwards we wished that we had taken the man's 'phone number for a progress report. The situation is still strange to us this day.

A MEDICAL CONUNDRUM

Len, the son-in-law of Geoff's brother Tom, received a heart transplant at the Harefield hospital Middlesex near London in 1989. Soon following the operation there seemed to be a continual threat to the success of this transplant in serious complications and there have been subsequent health problems, but by divine Grace he is alive as I write this story, approaching Christmas 2007. Len has baffled people by saying that the heart donor survived after giving his heart to Len! The answer is that Len's donor needed a new lung but a heart and lung must be excised, saved and transplanted together! So the donor's fit heart went to Len.The two men receiving donor organs were operated on at the same time by two different surgical teams So the deceased person gave life to two different people!

A SUMMARY

Some of the above stories of events cannot be explained by what is known of natural law; they point to a reality or world that is real but elusive. The contrast in the stories recounted tells us that there are helpful unseen influences but also dark or even dangerous unseen influences that are intermingled with our world. The Bible instructs us to fill our minds with good positive and loving thoughts that attract the good influences and energies from the unseen world. To replace doubt and fears with faith and confidence - to cultivate loving thoughts in place of hate and resentment for *like attracts like* - this is known to be a spiritual principle or law.

"Fix your thoughts on what is true and good and right. Think about things that are pure and lovely, and dwell on the fine, good things in others. Think about all you can to praise God for and be glad about." - These wise words were written in a letter to the Philippians Chapter 4 from verse 8 -The Living Bible Version.

Tragically, much that passes for entertainment on television flouts this wise advice. The violent sick murders and angry fights and quarrels shown into our homes feed the tendency for dark and violent thoughts in some maladjusted people. It cannot be denied that the style of some horrific murders have been inspired by what has been seen on video or TV. The young are easily influenced. How much healthier it is to use our spare time on activities that are creative or make us feel happier, more relaxed and optimistic.

CHAPTER EIGHT

On His Majesties Service In Egypt & Palestine 1945-48

As a free spirit and having enjoyed such a lot of free-roaming time in his life, the prospect of Army life filled Geoff with stomach churning horror! Happily blending Geoff into Service life was like trying to mix oil with water. This period in his life was tantamount to a prison sentence for him and made such a deep impression on him that he often refers to it and recounts the key events! Some men take to it like a duck to water; there are many positive advantages to Army life providing that you do not possess a naturally rebellious or strongly independent spirit! We shall place Geoff in the second class to avoid a domestic eruption here at home!

BRECON SOUTH WALES

When Geoff was called up at eighteen he started six weeks of intensive training at the Royal Welsh Fusiliers Army Training Camp, at Brecon S Wales. It was constructed mainly of wooden hut type buildings.

The day started with reveille at 6am. Lights went out at 10pm.

There were regular drills with full kit and weapons. There were extensive route marches producing blisters on tender feet unused to such vigorous exercise; it was not unusual for men to faint. The first quick march was four miles; the distance grew to ten miles. The practical studded army boots that were issued made Geoff recoil in horror, they seemed so heavy and unyielding; wearing these was an agony in itself until they were broken in, then Geoff realised what essential footgear they were.

There was the inevitable assault course; Geoff found climbing the vertical net the most difficult. The days were hectic; relaxing time was given in the evening except for rotated guard duty.

There was a competitive spirit between the several squads and their training Sergeants. Geoff's squad came out the best out of about half a dozen.

Geoff has slim feet with a very high instep that has reduced his choice of shoe style and caused occasional problems but he was classed as A1 meaning fully fit. Later when he was seen by an army doctor he commented on his feet surprised that he had been graded A1. He queried if he had suffered unduly wearing boots. He informed Geoff that strictly speaking he should have been classed as B1 and excused boots, root marches, guard duty and parades. Geoff, who has never been attracted to any competitive sports or physical disciplines and whose spirit of martyrdom has a genetically low calibration, met this news with deep dismay! Had he known this he would certainly have made an issue over his feet... Brave soul! Huh!

Medical treatments- One of the necessary preparations was a series of five vaccinations. They would stand in queues waiting their turn. Some of them collapsed to the floor as they watched the needles going into the flesh of their colleagues! Some of the lads had bad reactions as did Geoff. Sometimes arms and glands under the arm would become inflamed and very sore but training still had to continue!

After one vaccination Geoff started to feel unwell with headache, sweating and with a red rash on both feet and legs. He went to the medical centre and was seen by the medical orderly (a kind of nurse) he was quite young with limited experience.

He said, "You're in the wrong place, you should see a chiropodist." This sounded grossly inappropriate advice but he virtually staggered there as he did not have the strength to argue. The chiropodist took a look at Geoff's legs, went into the next room and came back with a thermometer and took Geoff's temperature. In shock he said, " Good Lord, you have a temperature of 104F!" - which is high -105F is a very dangerous sign.

Geoff knew no more from that point until he came round in a single-bed hospital ward. He had fainted and must have been unconscious for some time.

When he came round he made a shock discovery. He could not feel his arm and concluded that an amputation had taken place! Unconscious patients should be turned regularly to prevent the blockage of circulation, this had not been done. Fortunately with the onset of pins and needles the arm recovered despite the fact that this was the arm that had received the injection. He was in hospital over a week.

The hospital spell did not delay his training because he was doing well.

There was a dental department where teeth would be examined followed by immediate radical treatment without further ado! There was a row of about six dental chairs served by six dentists. There was a dreadful continuous chorus of crying, screaming, and shrieks of agony as fillings and extractions were carried out on a conveyor belt principle. Dentistry was not like the sophisticated and largely pain-free procedures of today. The sight of the old-time huge steel re-usable needle was enough to trigger a terror-provoked faint! Some times six noisy drills operating made the surgery sound more like a factory workshop!

Most of the lads waiting outside were trembling violently, faces ashen, waiting to enter the chamber of horrors! However Geoff boasts a filling today that originates from that time, sixty-three years ago! Fancy that now!

For decades Geoff would avoid dentists, well, until toothache forced the issue! He is fortunate to have strong teeth.

The Selection Board - All the young soldiers had attended a selection board to decide on their future placement. Geoff, answering routine questions and having some idea of what he wanted to do said that he would like to go into the REME (Royal Electrical Mechanical Engineers) this was noted.

A few days late he was given a travel warrant and information about his future posting.

AT CATTERICK N YORKSHIRE

This posting was to be with The Royal Signals at the Catterick Army Camp in North Yorkshire.

This posting was a big disappointment and seemed to bear no relationship to Geoff's expressed desire. However he received eleven weeks training in driving all types of vehicles and mechanical training.

There was instruction in map reading with a four-day map-reading trip at a time when roads signs had been removed and there were no street lights for it was still in the war blackout period. A compass helped them in combination with the map but the area was a confusion of country lanes. There were four men on this exercise in one vehicle - a 1500cwt Bedford canvas pick-up.

The time of year was November, and it was bleak and cold. They had to sleep in the canvas -topped pick-up -two at the front and two at the back on meagre rations. This experience gave a Geoff a permanent prejudice against Yorkshire that still clings to this day. Wild hedge-free moors hold no charm for Geoff.

An apple orchard was raided on one occasion to supplement their rations. But they were spotted and an irate farmer fired his 12bore gun, presumably into the air. There was the occasional cafe but the bill of fare that they could muster in that post war period was very limited.

One of the toughest exercises Geoff experienced was in a converted army ambulance with an instructor. It had been converted into an amphibian vehicle. It was designed to travel through high levels of water; there were no doors or windscreen, which could provide a way of escape A ramp had been created to drive down into water to drive up the other side. This was to mimic landing on seashore. The water completely covered the two men and in that condition the vehicle had to be driven several yards before climbing out! This taking place in a North Yorkshire November! Brrrh!

The instructor impressed upon Geoff the importance of keeping moving in first gear that was employed gently at the start. If the driver panicked underwater, escape was easily possible but the vehicle would have to be pulled out. Geoff was successful but not so every man, to the cold, wet discouragement of the instructor who would accompany several men in one training session. A warm shower and cup of tea was a most welcome finale to this exercise!

After four different postings in the UK he was chosen to go abroad December 1945 only one month after V. J. day that marked the end of the war with Japan. He was to sail on the converted passenger liner the S S Orion, a 24,000-ton ship. It was adapted for troop transport, to take them to foreign lands, a cargo of around 8,000 troops.

IN THE TRANSIT CAMP - OSSETT YORKSHIRE

The young soldiers were prepared for embarkation to their overseas posting. True to military procedure they were not told where, but the issue of tropical K.D., (meaning khaki drill) including bush hats signified that they were definitely not off to Siberia! A clue was given for on their kit bags and some equipment, was stencilled the letter H. Rumour had it that they were bound for Hong Kong or Haifa, Palestine. However, the kit was withdrawn to store when they were sent home for 14 days embarkation leave; it was not returned to them on return from leave to the Ossett camp, but the previous K. D. kit was changed to normal K.D. and the bush hats were not re-issued.

Hearse Driver - One day when Geoff was checking the details of his identity documents he noticed against the section *Employment* was typed - HEARSE DRIVER! It should have read -HORSE DRIVER! He never bothered to have it corrected - well - you could never tell what employment Geoff would take up next! Perhaps on demob he might well be a hearse driver, whether horse and carriage or modern automobile! For sure, there's no shortage of work in that field, after all, professionally speaking there is always a *lively* future in the 'dying' business!

THE TROOP SHIP SAILED FROM LIVERPOOL - CHRISTMAS EVE DAY!

Kit bags still bore the letter H. Most of those sailing were young inexperienced recruits.

By the inscrutable workings of the senior Army mind, the ship was set to sail at 12.45-pm Christmas Eve day! The Scottish Regiment to show the intensity of their disgust and displeasure, rioted; many of the rest of the lads soon followed suit! Many were jumping off the ship; many were throwing overboard whatever loose article or equipment they could grab.

The press arrived to record the disorder and excitement! The military police were called and they came in force, possibly 100 of them. Order was restored after the ship moved away from the dockside. Many were arrested.

After the ship set sail those arrested were given a choice to return to it on a pilot cutter or to face a military police charge on shore. The ship heaved to in order to pick up the men from the cutter. The men on board who did not know what was happening heard the engines stop and wildly thought that they were going to be allowed home for Christmas after all! No such luck! All the rioters were placed on a Charge. With typical Army logic, those who returned to the ship were confined to ship for seven days with fatigues! (Weren't they allowed to swim in the sea then?) The voyage actually took ten days! But their real punishment would be fatigues, meaning the dirty jobs and night tasks.

The boat sailed, full of shouting, cursing, disgruntled young men, hardly more than boys. What an ignominious start!

The pressmen, who sympathised with the lads, were very busy taking statements and photographs.

THE BAY OF BISCAY

Things fortunately settled down into a routine. That is, until the ship entered the Bay of Biscay! The weather turned foul, the wind blew, the rains lashed, the waves pounded the ship and the gigantic swell lifted the vessel for ever upwards as though in a lift... then it sank and sank, leaving stomachs behind...and hit the bottom of the waves as though striking solid ground with a fearsome noise and vibration. The ship rose and listed, to as much as 45 degrees. The propellers raced and vibrated as they came out of the water with the tossing and rolling of the ship in the heaving demented seas.

A great many were sick included the seasoned mariners, the regular crew.

The ship was tossing throughout a four-day storm. There was pure chaos on board -conditions became horrendous. Sleep was a near impossibility. The men slept in hammocks that swung as the ship rolled. They had to constantly protect themselves from banging each other and the roof!

Chaos Horrendous!

Men were vomiting in the sleeping decks. The storage of clothes and blankets become a vexed problem.

The 'ablutions' area, meaning washbasins and toilets (there were no showers) were an absolute nightmare. Waste from the toilets and basins sloshed backwards and forwards on the floor because it could not flow out of the ship as it was never on an even keel! ...And the men vomited everywhere ... Geoff remained unaffected –well, for a while! Unfortunately there were some women and children aboard, to see to their needs was a Herculean task! The memory of this nightmare trip would be deeply etched in their memory forever!

As well as other things, Geoff was appointed ship's Runner. His job was to pin notices on every notice board on the ship including on the bridge where the Captain and crew control the vessel. On one occasion when he visited the bridge instead of the normal crew of around four men, there was only one, struggling with the steering of the ship - though others were coming and going.

"Where's the rest of the normal crew?" Queried Geoff.

"Most of them are sick, *including* the Captain! Other crew members are having to double up because of crew sickness!" Came the reply!

Chaos Revolting!

Geoff entered the galley to update their notice board...another nightmare scene unfolded!

Down the galley to one side was the preparation area; down the other, the ovens, hotplates and equipment. The length appeared to be about 50yds. Stressed, sweating cooks and galley staff were darting this way and that, working swiftly, engaged in a bizarre battle, fighting with the equipment, trying to persuade it to stay on the work surfaces...And to keep the eggs in the colossal sloping pans on sloping stoves! They were losing the battle.

Geoff, stunned ...mesmerised ...watched eggs being scooped up off the galley floor and back into the frying pans! ...

But *who* wanted porridge, fried eggs and bacon anyway!?

Soon after this disturbing scene Geoff passed a man on deck eating a runny egg sandwich, egg yoke greasily running down his chin...while the storm raged and the ship heaved... that image was a view too much! Yuck! Geoff's 'internals' also gave up the unequal struggle...he too became a reluctant green-hued member of the company of disabled heaving rookies...!

As the storm coincided with the Christmas period, the galley staff, notwithstanding, in true indefatigable army style continued the sacrosanct army routines and busied themselves in their efforts to produce all the normal Christmas fare to include fried foods, fatty pork and the ubiquitous army lumpy, sugarless, watery porridge... and prunes!

THE CREATURES IN THE SEA MUST HAVE HAD A FEAST!

Eventually the storm subsided, as they entered the Mediterranean, the vessel was hosed down from top to bottom - all vents opened - most of the men recovered and normal life aboard ship resumed.

They were compensated for their recent misery in their enjoyment of the beautiful calm blue seas and warming December sun. Such stark contrast.

CHAOS UNNERVING

After the storm one of the corporals of Geoff's group questioned one of the experienced crew about the severity of the storm.

"Was it as serious as we thought? - Did we nearly come to grief?"

"It was the worst storm that I have ever encountered.... and yes, we were in *very* serious danger. It was a close thing"

Geoff felt very fortunate and somehow specially blessed that they had survived.

~

Some musings on how things and places are named: I wondered why the Pacific Ocean was so named which could be sorely misleading to the uninformed mariner! To quote from Chamber's dictionary published 1999 - 'Pacific Ocean' is so named because Magellan, the first European to sail on it, found it in calm weather'.

Supposing that the Bay of Biscay had been so hastily named! Today that portion of the seas could be called 'Sea of Tranquillity'! What a misnomer that would have been! - - - There is a moral in this story - how prone we are to labelling a person or situation on our first encounter, but we may have arrived on an off day - on an atypical time when temporary, hidden stressful pressures were distorting the picture!

~

DESTINATION REVEALED

The mystery of their destination was solved when they steamed into the Harbour of Port Said, Egypt. The ship was too large to dock so the men were transferred to landing barges.

A good sense of balance is required to descend a shaky metal ladder with only one free hand for grasping, and weighed down with more than a full kit. Fortunately no one fell in to the sea and they stepped into an amphibious craft that took them to the shore where they disembarked and were led to a transit camp, under canvas.

Lashed with whips -Whilst waiting for their turn to disembark from the ship the men spotted on the shore a number of coal barges being unloaded with a conveyer, or line, of dozens of men who were obviously convicts, or even slaves. They were in a continuous moving line zigzagging up and down a terraced path to load the coal into truck containers.

Two gangway planks connected the barge to the shore, fore and aft. One plank was to board the barge - the other to leave. Some of the men were in the normal Arab long -shirt style dress - others were bare to the waist Geoff first noticed the men going down to the barge - they had an old sack draped over one shoulder Each man coming off the barge carried a large wicker basket fully loaded with coal balanced on one shoulder; the purpose of the sack on the one shoulder became apparent. They were climbing up the bank to load the coal on to a truck; their faces were blackened with coal dust and streaked with sweat.

It was a disturbing scene for they were frequently lashed with whips by their guards

When the troops had disembarked they were led to rail cattle trucks fitted with wooden seats fitted across. The walls were wooden slats that gave some view of the surroundings. In one corner was a hole in the wooden floor used as a urinal. There was no screening.

At camp the men were divided into different regiments to move off to different locations. Geoff's Regiment spent just a half-day there.

At that time the British Army were in occupation in Egypt and the Suez Canal zone to protect the Canal for the use of the Allies. The Canal was constructed by and being run by the Suez Canal Company working with the Allies. But ten years later it was nationalised by Nasser, the Nationalist President of Egypt. In 1956 Anthony Eden declared war against Nasser to regain possession of the canal but the mission failed miserably.

THE FIRST CAMP

They arrived at a desert camp about 40 miles south of Cairo. It was all under canvas! They slept on ground sheets in tents that held six men. The lived like this for three months

In this period Geoff caught sand fly fever; symptoms were high temperature with flu' like symptoms which landed him in hospital. Then later he developed prickly heat that periodically returned for seven years. Urgent itching was a continual and distressing symptom requiring immediate relief.

Sanitary arrangements could not have been more basic.

The urinal was a piece of folded corrugated iron running down into a pipe that was buried into the sand. The lavatories were holes dug into the sand over which were placed large boards with holes in the middle of them. No water was accessible! Even the high-ranking men had nothing more civilised.

For personal washing - a row of enamel bowls on a long wooden bench with a single coldwater tap at one end coming from a storage tank. The shower consisted of a row of showerheads behind a canvas screen. The water flowed from a raised storage tank

Toasted weevils It was here that Geoff learned the serious value of toasted bread. The toasting was to kill the weevils! Flour was normally weevil infested.

One of the worst aspects of life in this camp was that most of the men had to do guard duty every other night. The shifts were organised in two-hour stints with four-hour breaks between. There were four men on each shift patrolling the four sides of the square camp. The camps were at risk of being robbed or seriously attacked.

THE SECOND CAMP

The next camp to which the regiment moved was a permanent camp based at Maadi, near Cairo. Occasionally the men would spend their off duty time in Cairo. Italian prisoners of war were still working in this camp

THE FINAL CAMP

This was based at El Balyana - an ex RAF camp. It was alongside the Suez Canal that was just half a mile away. From a distance it looked like ships were sailing through the sand

The Sweetwater canal was not far away. This was obviously named with tongue-in-cheek. The canal was used for everything! Whatever one does in the bathroom and laundry room was done in the canal! All this in no particular order or place and the water appeared slow moving. Animals too were washed in it. It was unnervingly foul and stinking. In the evening the ammonia smell that it emitted made ones eyes smart. Army seniors said that if anyone chanced to fall in they would require seventeen different inoculations! This was in1945.

Facilities were rather better at this camp. The men's lines were still tents but they were fixed over dugouts making a safer situation and with low bunks as at Maadi.

A TRIP TO PALESTINE

Officially Officers were not allowed to drive in the Suez Canal zone. Designated drivers would drive them, but they did not adhere to this rule.

Trips to Palestine required that they keep Sten guns on their lap whilst travelling because of terrorists planning reprisals. It was the time Jewish people were starting to come back to Palestine.

Geoff normally drove the Officer Commanding, Ken another driver normally drove the Commanding Officer - he was the most senior Officer in the Camp. They were asked to prepare for a 4-day pleasure trip to Palestine through the Sinai desert, driving the OC and the CO in their respective jeeps. Geoff was proud of his jeep and took very good care of it. He shone up the metal parts and cleaned up the bodywork. It may have been the smartest vehicle on the camp.

After departing and travelling some distance they passed a REME Camp. Geoff was thankful at the time that he had not been posted with them as they were miles from anywhere in the middle of the desert.

On the way to Palestine the CO stopped and his driver approached Geoff's jeep. Their plan was for the two drivers to use Ken's jeep, with trailer. The two officers then claimed Geoff's jeep, much to Geoff's dismay, and told the drivers to follow, but they intentionally moved off so fast that soon they were out of sight.

After some distance a tyre on the trailer blew out and the drivers were forced to stop. The only option was to sit and wait until the officers realised that they were missing to come back looking for them. They waited 1.5hours and sure enough the Officers returned. Between them they hoisted the trailer on to the back of the jeep across the backbench.

Eventually their destination for three nights came in view, the Army camp in Palestine, Officers could make arrangements with other camps to stay for a break, it was a useful place for sightseeing; the field and trees were good to see after all that sand. The drivers were shown their parking place and barracks; the officers went to their quarters.

On the morning of the return journey the CO's driver was reprimanded because he had failed to fill up with petrol. The officers had filled up Geoff's jeep. This should have been done the night before.

The trip over and back to base camp Ken was immediately put on a charge for his delay in filling up with petrol. His rank was 'corporal' and he was stripped of his stripes and returned to the ranks. He was demoted from driving the CO. Considering that they were on a pleasure trip and there was no danger threatening, this charge was a highhanded act. The charge went on his record. Some officers could be very arrogant and officious, enjoying flaunting their authority.

At a later time the OC sent for Geoff for a similar trip but Geoff made a stipulation that he Geoff would drive the jeep throughout, according to army rules.

Geoff said "My jeep has not been the same since that trip," It had started burning oil belching out fumes.

End of interview: then came an order to report to the RSM

Geoff was called to the office of the Regimental Sergeant Major who was obviously set to soft-soap Geoff. His atypical manner was warm and coaxing -

"Sit down I want a chat with you my lad ...Now what's all this about your refusing to allow an Officer to drive?"

But Geoff, furious about the Corporal's demotion and knowing the rules, stood his ground. The Sergeant's mood was somewhat changed on dismissing Geoff,

"You'd better watch your step from now on, my lad, I'll be keeping an eye on you." Fortunately there were no repercussions. Another driver with jeep was found.

SOME FRIEND!

One of Geoff's friends Taff, from Pontypridd, S Wales, was asked to baby sit one evening at Christmas for his Major the OC who was posted in married quarters with his wife and family of two young boys. Taff asked Geoff to join him. This was in Ism'iliya, Egypt, north of Cairo

When they arrived to baby sit the officer invited them to enjoy the Christmas fare laid out in the living room. Unfortunately Taff over indulged in everything! He refused to heed Geoff's warnings. When he got fresh he kept visiting the children's bedroom putting his face round the door and stupidly saying,

"Are you all right boys?"

Geoff, who could not control him followed him .The bedroom was just off the living room and Geoff could see the staring eyes of the scared boys sat up in bed in the dim light.

Quietness was called for, but not surprisingly, in due course, Taff broke out into the un-modulated 'singing of the sozzled' Geoff was becoming increasingly anxious.

Then Taff was sick on the living room floor rug! Poor old Geoff had the task of cleaning up the mess and that caused *him* to be sick! Fortunately he managed to reach the sink - then he had this mess to rinse away. He was doing this when, horrors, the OC and his wife returned! Geoff in acute embarrassment apologised profusely. Taff was lolling in a chair grinning stupidly. The Officer was clearly shocked. His wife, no doubt anxious to get rid of the lads said -

"Not to worry, I'll clean things up."

She then rushed to the children anxious about their welfare. They were awake and more or less OK

Geoff had to bodily haul the legless Taff into his jeep.

Taff was up before the Officer the next morning who tore him off a strip but as it was not official business he could not punish him.

THE CRASH

There was an incident in the Egyptian deserts that is imprinted on Geoff's mind forever!

He was travelling in open 3ton Chevrolet truck with 20 other men. It was a dark night and the lights were weak due to a charging fault - there was no moon. The driver was going too fast for the conditions. The desert road had no visible boundaries - the edges merged into the sand of the desert. Occasionally there were trees and boulders at the edges. The men were seated in rows on fold-up wooden chairs. They felt neither comfortable nor safe. The floor of the truck was metal with nothing to stop the chairs sliding should there be an accident.

Geoff is and always was a careful driver and felt very uneasy. He leant forward and spoke in the ear of the man in front who was just behind the rear cab window,

"Tell the driver that there is an army vehicle, a Bedford pick-up behind us, it has good lights; tell him to flag down the pick-up to arrange to follow it"

The curt rejoinder came. "Bill's the driver. He knows what he's doing"

Geoff slumped back on his chair disheartened and tense. The vehicle behind them overtook and sped away.

Ten minutes later the inevitable happened.The truck crashed head on... to nobody knew what! The men were propelled forward into a mangled heap of bodies, limbs and chairs. Many screamed in pain and fear.All were injured, some badly with broken bones... there was blood... but fortunately there were no fatalities. Geoff discovered that his back was deeply bruised and also his legs. (He suffered from shock for many years afterwards - one outcome was a fear of wobbly chairs!)

As soon as the vehicle, which was open to the skies, jarred to a sudden halt Geoff felt a shower of something damp and soft splattering over him. The other lads were similarly affected...then ...they became conscious of a grossly foul smell!

"Oh, shit!" Some of them cried...No kidding ...they were spot on! ...Yuck -they were all covered in camel dung!

The truck had left the road completely and had run into a stationary open topped lorry that was parked off the road for the night. Two Arabs were in charge. In the dim light, they were seen running for all they were worth into the desert, terrified! In their flowing off-white Arab dress they looked like agitated ghosts in the darkness of the night! It was discovered that the men were driving a lorry piled high with camel dung, used for building huts, and they were sleeping underneath...The mind boggles...!

Sleeping as usual in the normal deep stillness of the desert night the men must have thought that the end of the world had begun!

The impact had catapulted the noxious cargo up into the air! - The soldiers were in civvies -grey flannels and white shirts, spattered with blood ...and dung! What a bizarre mix!

The men had to painfully tumble out on to the desert floor to sit or lie in the sand until another army jeep *just happened* to come along. There was no way of calling for help - they waited 2.5hrs until a jeep approached. The driver saw hands waving in the road - the headlight beams picking up the white of their shirts but he hesitated thinking it was an ambush.... But he was their human *angel of deliverance*. - Their rescue lorry arrived - 1.5hrs later.

Tender loving care was in seriously short supply on return to their camps; they had to report for sick parade at eight o' clock the next morning! Except for the seriously wounded they were prescribed M and D - meaning *medicine and duties*. The next day, the men were shattered, shocked, aching and in pain - tired and miserable...very!

DRY HUMOUR

The sergeant major inspecting the troops on parade enjoyed dry humour. If someone were badly shaven he would bark -

"Stand closer to the razor!"

To another he would bawl - "Am I hurting you?" The guilty soldier fearfully wondering what he meant would ask,

"What do you mean, Sir?"

The sergeant would stand behind him, "I am standing on your hair!"

PERSONALITIES

What an assortment of personalities Geoff met in the Army; some took well to Army life - some like Geoff, did not. Geoff hated the regimentation especially the mindless 'bull' - routines that had little purpose other than breaking self will or knocking the spiky corners off a rebel spirit. Obedience and team spirit is of paramount importance when on active duty.

There was **Tom** who went around in an overcoat in the hot desert climate trying to appear mentally unhinged, he wore it even on a group leisure trip to the Great Pyramid. He climbed through the stifling poorly lit claustrophobic passages with the rest of the men - still wearing his overcoat. The ploy achieved nothing.

Then there was **Dennis** who could wake up with one eye open, and provided that he did not open the other eye he could easily resume his sleep!

Geoff shared a tent with four other men for about 18months.

There was **Johnny**, a nice guy with stinking feet! His hygiene routine was good but he could not beat his problem; his tent mates insisted that he hung his socks outside the tent!

Roger was a good chap but suffered severe epileptic fits, which were quite alarming and disruptive to the other lads in the tent barracks. It was one of the mysteries of Army life that such a disability was disregarded! There was a way of warding off a fit - if he was administered a drink of water without delay this would avert an attack but this was not always possible. Once he collapsed on to the sand on the weekly pay parade and started fitting. The sergeant on parade gave orders to ignore him because it was thought that he was a malingerer. Fortunately the orderly officer came over to investigate and the soldiers reassured him that the man was genuine. A fit began by grunting when his muscles would start stiffening, if water was not administered it would develop into a full-blown episode and would frighten the life out of his tent companions. He would thresh about vigorously and as he had a top bunk this could be dangerous.

Here was a man with a genuine problem but had been declared A1 - the highest fitness class.

Skip - the nickname of another tent mate - was a very lean individual with red hair and so was very sensitive to the sun! Egypt was hardly a fitting setting for this man whose one prevailing obsession was to escape direct sunlight!

Harry, from Suffolk, was the eldest of the group and was an ace player at draughts; but to his great delight Geoff beat him on one occasion. There was a strange accident involving Geoff and Harry. The two men were on 'sandbag' duty - this involved filling sacks with sand to make protective walls around the tents. Not surprisingly they were doing their own tent first before those of the officers. The sandbags were to protect against sandstorms. When the huge bails of empty sandbags were opened it involved pushing a steel pin out of a metal holding strap. The pins were over an inch long with a quarter inch diameter.

In the typical competitive mood of youth, with every pin that the lads handled they played a game - it was hitting the pins with a hammer into the desert to see who could project one the farthest. The pin would give a rather satisfactory pinging sound, like the ricochet of a bullet, as it travelled through the air at speed.

Once when it was Geoff's turn, the pinging sound came to an abrupt end. He turned to Harry, "That one didn't go very far!"

No reply, dead silence. No Harry! Geoff looked down and saw his mate flat and inert on the ground between two walls of sandbags.

"I've killed him!"

The initial dreadful quiet was quite literally a *stunned silence!* Geoff had knocked Harry out cold! By a fluke, the steel pin had struck Harry on the temple and he fell down like a ninepin. Geoff rushed to him in fear but Harry came round and his first reaction was rage at the thought of his brush with death. An enraged Harry was a scary prospect indeed because he was a tough, strong guy.

No more sandbag duties were performed *that* day. Happily, there were no ill repercussions, neither concerning Harry's health nor in their relationship.

AN EXOTIC PET

The lads captured a chameleon, a type of lizard; they could be found in the sand. They reminded Geoff of prehistoric creatures. Their four feet are pads with a thumb like projection. Their movement is extremely slow and deliberate, their eyes independently moving and scanning all the time; the eyes were a source of fascination. The eyeball is covered with a skin with the actual eye being a black pinpoint in the middle.

The specimen the men caught was about ten inches long including the long tail. They erected a rope between poles across their tent and tied string to the creature's legs so that it could walk up and down the rope but not escape. They found him to be useful in capturing and eating flying insects including locusts nearly three inch in length. He would open his mouth very slowly and then his long sticky tongue would dart out swiftly to catch its prey. When there was no prey to catch, the creature would gently rock to and fro until something appeared.

They tested his ability to change to the colour of his environment. Anything dyed in one colour he would mimic convincingly. Obviously they are a sand colour in their natural habitat. They placed him in a white bowl. This must have been too drastic, too stark- it made him angry! probably because he was afraid of the grossly strange and unfamiliar environment. Placed on tweed material he adopted a sort of mottled design.

SHIP AHOY!

On the second trip to Egypt, after home leave, Geoff palled up with a man from Wales nicknamed Taff. On the newly boarded ship SS Georgic, at Southampton, they were strolling on the deck when a very senior officer of the crew appeared, walking towards them his smart uniform festooned with gold braid and brass buttons. The imposing uniform was topped by a blue/white peak cap on his head

The two young soldiers crisply stopped to attention, army style and saluted.

Taff with his usual laid back approach greeted him with -'Ay mate, what's the name of this boat?"

Geoff winced silently. The tall officer stopped dead and with chilled expression looked down at Taff. He reprimanded him in powerful sonorous tones -

"This, my son, is **not** a boat!" His chest swelled as he drew in an indignant breath! -"It is a ship! You will do well to remember that...And I am not your 'mate'...I am *the Captain*!"...

Stunned, the two sprung to attention again; Geoff did the apologising and with their best salute dismissed themselves.

THE LONG DREARY WAIT

Drawing near to the time for being demobbed Geoff was working as batman/driver for an officer named Captain Christie, until he - Captain Christie - was demobbed; somehow Geoff was not drafted to different duties apart from the routine drills and guard duties; he was quite adept at dodging the worst positions, and mooched inconspicuously around the camp waiting for the vessel that would take him to home and freedom!

By 'dodging the column' with consummate skill he blended into the shadows and thus managed to escape duties! For 3months in fact. A Captain Gort finally spotted Geoff in the orderly room where Geoff was enquiring about his delayed demob home-sailing for his name had not appeared on the appropriate list. It is not the most fortunate turn of fate to be allotted a surname starting with 'W'!

He was immediately given fresh duties for the final ten days.

Geoff had been told by his training Sergeant at Brecon Barracks S Wales that he had the makings of a good soldier because when he became interested in a job he gave it his best, but his inner eye was always focused on the day of discharge!

When it was Geoff's time to go home an administrative mix up meant that his name was left off the appropriate list for his home trip. He missed the first sailing with all the mates of his squad as a result. In great frustration he had to spend a further ten days doing normal duties around the camp continuing with his normal driving and escort tasks. Before his mates left for home Geoff came in for a lot of flack and teasing. It was not so funny for Geoff; he did not share the humour. He saw his pals jubilantly board ship and away ... and he was left behind!

Those ten days felt to be the loneliest, longest and dreariest period of his life.

Note - The spelling or naming of some places may have been changed over time

CHAPTER NINE

It Must Have Been An Angel

Looking back, Geoff can recall several occasions when he could have been killed and feels that there was Divine or angelic intervention. Either, or, it amounts to the same thing. Either he was saved for a purpose, or it was his deep unspoken inner faith that was operating on his behalf. This chapter recounts the main events of near misses.

THE HEAD-ON CRASH THAT DID NOT HAPPEN

Geoff has had an ongoing relationship with vehicles - and boats - beginning early in his adult life, perhaps from around the age of twelve. This story happened when he was the personal chauffer to a Mrs Hatton, an elderly widow lady, the owner of a firm contracted to run four large works' canteens in a wide area.

They were driving down a straight stretch of road with a lorry approaching fairly fast on the other side. The road was not wide enough for three vehicles to come abreast. Then to his horror, another lorry behind the approaching one started to overtake and he would have had to use Geoff's side of the road. Geoff knew that there was no breaking distance to avert a head-on. In that instance he had no recollection what was on the side of the road, whether dyke, ditch, building or bank - sheer face or sheer drop!

But suddenly, he felt as though his steering wheel was taken over by an invisible hand; quicker than thought, the wheel spun to send the car off the road and harmlessly on to a grassy verge. Almost instantaneously, the car rocked with the pressure of air as the overtaking lorry sped past. His employer gasped in relieved shock.

"Oh! Driver Wood that was a bit of brilliant quick thinking! We could have been killed!"

He had sensed the help of an unseen agent.

Note - Heavy industry has disappeared or dwindled down to small-scale operations since those days. Two of the firms that Mrs Hatton was involved in were the huge Whitehead's Iron and steel works and the complimentary firm, Goddens sited adjacently. Both were situated to the West of Newport. The first was a steel rolling mill; the latter fabricated steel structures of the ilk of bridges and car body parts. This was before the huge undertaking of the construction of the Llanwern Steel Works near Newport. This massive steel works, as it was, is now dead.

Eye to eye with a large steaming locomotive buffer -

Again with his passenger, employer Mrs Hatton - who always travelled along side the driver - Geoff approached a well known manned large mainline railway crossing of four parallel tracks: he was slowing down when he was beckoned forward by the signal man controlling the gate. He was leaning on the open gate. So naturally

Geoff continued driving and was crossing the first set of lines when they both heard the almighty squeal of breaks of a locomotive which was approaching the crossing on the same track.

Geoff automatically slammed on the cars brakes and suddenly there was a loud hiss of steam that covered the car, and they braced themselves for a terrible crushing impact. Mrs Hatton, who had a heart condition, screamed out loud in fear.

When the steam cleared they realised with immense relief that the locomotive had been able to stop just in time with one large metal bumper the size of a large dinner plate resting a couple of inches away from the driving door window, just inches from Geoff's face

The engine driver scrambled down from the hissing locomotive and came rushing to the car as did the signalman. They ran on either side of the car, concerned for the welfare of the occupants.

Mrs Hatton, in her naturally cultured tones addressing the crossing's operator, spluttered - "You've *really* upset me! I am a heart sufferer and you could have killed my driver and me, you careless man!"

Geoff, in that wild rage that is a frequent accompaniment to severe shock, exploded with somewhat less refinement -"You bloody idiot! What were you thinking of? I've a good mind to report you!" Subsequently he did not.

Mrs Hatton was shaking with shock and needed a stiff drink on arrival at home. Happily, she suffered no lasting ill effects.

This crossing, carrying the fast rail line between London and Cardiff, was approached very gingerly from then on!

Analysing the carelessness that caused the incident - it seems that the signalman had wrongly assessed the speed and distance of the engine. Had the engine been coupled to carriages no doubt he would have used more caution.

A STEP TOO FAR!

Geoff was high up a ladder painting his house - perhaps he had reached out too far, a common error in using ladders. But suddenly, the ladder moved sideways and swivelled right round.

Geoff found himself on the underside of the ladder clinging on to its rungs Fortunately the ladder decided to stay put as he gingerly climbed down, heart in mouth!

On reaching the ground he thought, "H'm ...Another near miss! ...Another lucky escape!"

There were several scary incidents in his Army days.

Geoff is narrating the following incident –

AMBUSHED BY WILD CHILDREN

Whilst serving in the Army two soldier friends and I were enjoying some free time - walking along the main street of Cairo, Solomon Pasha. It was just after the war and things were tense at that time. Many local people were suspicious of the British presence, although the Army used local labour to do many jobs in the Camp for they were glad of the employment.

We accidentally wandered down a side street - failed to see the notice that said -

OUT OF BOUNDS TO ALL SERVICE PERSONNEL -

It was one of many notices, placed by the Army that appeared down all the side streets leading to where the local people lived.

After about 50yards down the street we were quickly surrounded by half a dozen young Arab children who came begging with hands all over us and into our pockets.

Beggars were mostly everywhere; it was a way of life for many - especially for the many pathetically disabled people. A good number had disabled legs or no legs and would propel themselves around on a skateboard type of contraption.

We knew that we were now in an unprotected and vulnerable situation that had the potential of becoming dangerous...We knew that if we did not respond to their pleas things could get nasty. The people were pathetically poor which drove them to desperate means and the children were aggressive to acquire what they needed. Pens, watches, cash and whatever could be grabbed would disappear. We were more concerned about our military documents that we kept in a breast pocket. However, I had sewn an inner pocket to my uniform and kept my papers safe there. Children make excellent pickpockets and the locals could speak sufficient English to communicate.

In the commotion one little boy accused me of taking his money and placing it in my pocket. I had felt the hand of this boy enter my trouser pocket that in fact was empty; no doubt the boy felt thwarted at finding nothing. I pulled out the lining of my pocket to prove my innocence, but I knew that I was being tricked and compromised.

We soldiers had already experienced the aggression of the shoe-shine boys - that if we did not submit to the service they offered, they were likely to throw the black liquid polish all over our army uniform. A cringing toe-curling prospect!

Our fear mounted when we became aware that an adult audience was silently watching. Shaking inside, we wondered whatever was going to happen next…But timely deliverance suddenly appeared - in the person of a strongly built, fearsome looking six- foot-plus Arab man carrying a large long whip. He walked towards us, cracked the whip and facing the children gave a powerful verbal command in Arabic. Like magic the children melted away - we wish that our police were so on hand! -The whip wasn't a bad idea either - *because it worked!* Its effect was instant!

We stood transfixed as he came nearer...wondering... shaking. He glared at us in annoyance and no doubt disgust at our carelessness, we quivered in our boots. Despite our fear he nevertheless came as an angel of deliverance disguised as a human, for the time of his appearance was so apt. But, moving towards us, his glowering eyes focusing on us like a laser beam, his mouth hard and forbidding, we felt new terror. Then a few paces from us he stretched out his arm pointing to the way out and again in a thunderous voice of command the man bellowed -

"GO!" ... And we certainly went! ...Phew!!

A HEAVENLY SHOWER

This event occurred much later than the previous ones. It involved me.

My mother had celebrated her Century. The party had taken place in the residential Home situated in Bradford Yorkshire that had been her home for some years. I was born and brought up in a village on the country outskirts of Bradford, just a hike from Haworth of Bronte family fame.

It was January 11th 1999. We left for home at 7pm evening. The night sky was clear but with no moon. Our journey would take about 2hrs 30mins, to take us to near LLanymynech, just over the border from England. We were between addresses staying in a holiday cottage.

Several days previous to this there had been heavy snowfalls. The snow had mostly melted in a short warmer spell but on this particular evening the cold was quite intense. The water in the bottle for washing the car windscreen was frozen, probably in the tubes too. The roads were very dirty because of the gritting. We presumed that after travelling a good few miles the problem would resolve ...but it did not.

The M62 motorway took us over the Pennine Range and is very well lit so we managed quite well, Geoff driving, despite a film of dust and grime on the windscreen. We stopped two or three time to clean the screen. On one occasion we stopped at a Service Station to bring some warm water from the loo block to clean the windscreen.

Some miles past the Manchester area the powerful lights suddenly came to an end. We moved into the slow lane, to stay there. Apart from the stars, the darkness was deep.

'I'm going to have to get out frequently to clean the glass,' I thought to myself, 'but we don't have water on board! Oh dear!'

Almost simultaneously, Geoff uttered a spontaneous prayer, "Oh Lord, we could do with some rain!"

A mighty deluge of water immediately hit the windscreen, I instinctively shrunk back... it was such a dramatic impact! The glass was saturated and was completely cleaned. It was a miracle but not yet finished. - For the rest of the 90min journey, *the windscreen remained clean* and we had no further anxiety.

There was *absolutely no physical explanation* for this perfectly timed gift of water. Truly we had been *blessed by a miracle* for which we both gave our humble thanks to God.

~

WHERE KNOWLEDGE FAILS FAITH CAN TAKE OVER

Geoff and I have learned to believe by much personal evidence and the testimony of countless others that the kind of loving protection recounted above is what our heavenly father would love to give us in dangerous situations, through the ministry of his angels. He has shown us his sacrificial and forgiving love and evidence of the possibility of life after death, shown through the life, suffering, death and rising back to life of Jesus of Nazareth.

It is faith in God's available Goodness and Love, coupled with a desire to please Him and develop a relationship with Him that releases his Hand of Blessing on our behalf.

We need the humility to acknowledge that the human mind and miniscule knowledge available to it, will never fathom life's more complex mysteries nor find totally satisfactory answers to the vexed problems of agonising pain and the seeming injustices of this life.

Some hard-to-define and difficult-to-categorise evidence of unseen realities has been tapped, recorded, photographed, or whatever, in 'psychic laboratories'.

But not the finest laboratory instrument, nor telescope nor microscope, can convincingly penetrate that subtle yet dynamic - *world within this world.*

Researchers are working to understand the energies of another kind of reality - *within our world.* Some believe that the more sensitive 'eye' of the camera has picked up and recorded spiritual light and even spirit or ghost forms.

But how do you measure and tabulate the power of a personal faith? There is evidence in plenty, but scientific proof is elusive.

It takes a step into the dark, by faith, to swing open a door to enter a new dynamic world of Light - on the spiritual plane.

"Are they not all ministering spirits (angels) sent forth to serve, for the sake of those who are to obtain salvation?" Hebrews 1:14

~

CHAPTER TEN

What A Laugh! The World Of Humour

OFTEN UNEXPECTEDLY IN EVERYDAY LIFE there is a hilarious incident, a comical or incongruous situation, someone drops a clanger, or, one can see the funny side of a mishap or embarrassing situation. Seeing the funny side of life helps us to keep things in balance, relieves tension and protects us from going over the edge in situations that make no sense or justice. This chapter recounts varied samples.

Geoff narrates the following incidents-

THE WOOD AXE 'WARRIOR'

There was the time - around the age of seven - when I became very nervous and jittery as a result of sneaking in the cinema to watch scary adult films. My older sister Joyce used to make me worse by teasing me - they do don't they? - I mean, older sisters and brothers - they have a cruel streak!

There was one dark evening when I was climbing the stairs to bed when I fancied that I saw a ghost or something more substantial on the landing. There was no handy electric switch in those days. Stairs and landings could be very dark and forbidding places for the young and imaginative.

I thought I saw a white face showing up in the gloom. I screamed and nearly tumbled back down the steps in a panic to rush to Mum.

"Mum! There's somebody up there!" I gasped, in a stage whisper.

"Oh! We must get some help!"

Mum tended to be on the nervous side in this respect and enlisted the help of a neighbour.

This obliging lady dramatically gathered up a wood axe and rushed over the road from her cottage, courageously ready to do battle with the intruder.

But phantoms of the imagination need no wood-axe to disperse them! There was nothing there.

THE MONSTER ... THE TOAD, WHAT A BLOOMING SHAME!

I kept a favourite toad, named Hopalong. He was a magnificent specimen of his species - *large* you might say! The 'pride of the fleet' as it were ... needing two hands to hold him! Even I, as a young 'David Attenborough' in the making, was afraid of him when I first discovered him in a local pond, but I became the proud 'keeper' of Hopalong and soon grew quite 'affectioned' towards him. I kept him in the walled yard/garden at the rear of the house with a sunken water filled tin bath at his disposal; he was not a lonely soul for he had many companions at hand including minnows, tadpoles and various water- borne insects - thanks to me!

Mostly everyone had outside lavatories in those days. The neighbour's loo was alongside the dividing wall, which was a metre high. Very often the door would be left open to admit some light for there was a sufficient amount of privacy.

Natural stone walls pose little problem for frogs and toads, I often had to retrieve my 'family' from neighbour's gardens, so whether they liked it or not the neighbours were forced to be partakers in my passion for these little amphibians - or monsters, depending on one's view point! Mum got weary of people complaining about the anti social interests of her son!

One day the neighbour, Edie, a rather small thin frail woman, went into her loo - Seconds later, Mum and I heard an almighty shriek coming from the neighbour's garden. Mum rushed out and looked over the wall into the loo - - Oh my! What a sight!

Edie was standing balanced on the loo seat with her bloomers around her ankles! She was pointing down at the floor, eyes wide in fear,

"Look! Look!" She screamed.

Then Mum saw my proud possession on the loo floor just in the entrance of the toilet facing Edie and as it seemed to her eying her with his large yellow eyes, silently, and to the terrified eye - blinking menacingly...!

HORRORS! She was actually enthroned on the loo at the time of his grand entrance! The door was partly open when the prized toad hopped into the doorway! The incident didn't do much for my reputation! Come to think of it...it did a lot! But in the strongest negative sort of way!

Cash was very hand to mouth in those times; the pawnshops were very busy. Debt was a constant nightmare so it was not unusual for people to hide behind locked doors when the rent man or other tradesmen called for their legitimate payments

I'm not here; I'm somewhere else -

On one occasion when the insurance man came for the weekly payment of 2d - old money. Mum instructed me to go to the door and tell him that she was not in! So, dutifully, with my instruction carefully in mind I opened the door - the man said, "I'm from the Pru." (Prudential Insurance Co. a widely used company in those days) I briskly replied, "My mother's just told me to tell you that she's not in!" Oh! Some mothers do 'ave 'em!
With a wry smile he replied. "Tell your mother - who's not in ... that I'll soon call again." And he left.
Guess what Mum, cringing pitifully, said to that!

Now you see it ... Now you don't -

The coalman called on his usual weekly round with his normal alerting bellowing call, "Coal!"

Mum told me to go out and instruct him to empty a one - hundred - weight bag in to the cellar, which he promptly did. There was still a little coal left in the cellar. He stood outside waiting for payment. Again I was sent out to do the dirty work, which was to tell him that payment would be made next week. Credit was unobtainable in those cash impoverished days.

With a loud derisory grunt the coal merchant strutted back into the cellar and shovelled all the coal back into the bag, including the precious bit that had still been there! And promptly left.

Another coal merchant was duly found.

The practical joke -

Most children love playing pranks and jokes on people.

I acquired a trick nail. It was a nail with two bends in it so that you could rest a finger on it to give the illusion that the nail had passed through the finger. The illusion was made complete by a piece of gory coloured stained cotton wool attached. It was most authentic looking. I went rushing into the house hugging the finger with my sister aiding and abetting the prank.
My mother gasped. "Oh my goodness! Come to the sink, perhaps we can pull it out." She was truly shocked.
I kept up the pretence until we reached the tap. She was not amused!

Listening at the keyhole -

I remember one time when we were sharing a house in Newport with stepfather Bill's younger brother Alf, and his wife and daughter. This involved sharing kitchen and bathroom. One day, Alf and his wife were having a row in their living room, the door of which opened on to the communal hall. Mum heard them and went into the hall to listen to discover what the bone of contention was. Naturally, she would wonder if her family were the cause of the vexation. She had her ear against the door to eavesdrop, a quick-escape route being an adjacent pantry.

Being a cheeky thirteen-year-old when I found her in this compromising stance, for devilment I loudly chided - "Mum! Stop listening".

Mum froze and then gesticulated wildly in fright and embarrassment to shut me up. My sister Joyce, behind our living room door heard all and collapsing in mirth stifled her giggles behind her hand!

Fortunately, later, we all had a good laugh about it and no harm was done to family relationships.

~

Comment- In times of fear and tension any humorous trigger can release a safety valve of unrestrained laughter for merriment releases nervous tension in conditions of stress, danger and war. When I told Geoff that I was going to include the following somewhat vulgar anecdote he grimaced in apprehension.

"Aw ... yer not going to include *that !* ... are yer?"

But it is a very poignant human tale, portraying the paradoxical mix of everyday down-to-earth events and humour, coincidentally with the grim realities of violence and death. - A kind of bathos.

~

The midnight trumpet call! -

It was a clear summer's night during the war. The siren had sounded the warning of enemy approach. It was customary to go to the shelters for safety but on this occasion because it was such a lovely night dimming the sense of danger and somewhat distancing the grim reality of war, the five of us loitered by the gate - Mum, my sister Joyce, Aunty Minnie and her daughter Mildred and myself. - Anyway, a sojourn in those dim, damp, crowded shelters was certainly not a welcome escape.

The scatter of people to the communal shelters when the siren sounded had its comical side. Women, mostly the mature, would rush out of the house in their nightdresses clutching their clothes with corsets rolled up under the arm! It was certainly more judicious to grab these items - like glasses and dentures, rather than a jewel case or family heirloom! - If indeed they possessed any such thing that was not already residing in the pawnshop (even wedding rings were pawned) One young woman appeared in her wedding dress - using it as a nightdress!

We were watching the searchlights noiselessly roving the night sky for enemy aircraft when the unexpected happened.

Everything was dead silent; the atmosphere was growing acute with that still, tense, fearful expectation of the approach of danger – the deadly enemy bombers. Ears were alert waiting to pick up their heavy powerful droning as they carried the weight of their killer missiles.

The cautious ones were already settled in the shelters.

There was housing on each side of the road; a lone man appeared steadily walking on the opposite pavement. I noticed this man's dress; his dark corduroy trousers were tied below the knee with string. He was wearing boots and a well-worn unfastened jacket and buttoned waistcoat. His battered brimmed hat was of a kind of high-top variety - he was quite unaware of our presence for without a word or movement we had been scanning the skies in solemn expectant mood because of the warning siren.

Sirens had a sad and sombre wailing sound - churning up a feeling of dread and foreboding in the pit of the stomach.

'Who is going to get it tonight?' would be the unspoken question.

Suddenly, a l-o-n-g, loud reverberating trumpet-like sound rudely shattered the silence! The man, with notable lack of inhibition, had broken wind!! ...

It was a rather superior, unsurpassable example of the genre! Without altering his pace he just went on walking...Quite amazing what the human body is capable of!

We were all transfixed in silent, stunned and somewhat embarrassed surprise ...it was such an incongruous incident for the occasion!

Then ...Minnie exclaimed, "The dirty old bxxxxr!"

That did it... the high tension of the moment was gone in a flash! ALL five of us collapsed and were bent over in helpless hysterics!

With our hands on our mouths we stifled the noise of our merriment until the man was out of sight. Geoff developed a 'laughter pain' in his tummy.

("It was a right old snorter!" Geoff remembers, laughing. "Before or since, I have never heard anything to match such a' performance'!")

On a serious note –

Some minutes later that night we saw the enemy planes picked up by the strong roving beams of the searchlights and the Beaufort Guns opened fire on them. The bombers that night targeted the industrial sites in Newport, some less than a mile from where we lived but instead of hitting one of their intended targets, the Royal Ordinance Factory, the bombs demolished a row of terraced houses killing ten people. More bomb damage was done around Cardiff and Swansea.

There was an awful fluke tragedy that night; the hand of Destiny, or whatever, singled out just one house and one family for complete annihilation...but *not* by an enemy bomb.

One enemy bomber plane was shot down - not in the many acres of farmland and country around, but squarely on to one house. It was a stately residence in large grounds in a locality of similar properties - tragically, a whole three-generation family named

Philips, was wiped out! They owned a large thriving tobacconist/ newsagent shop in central Newport.

What curious misfortune - and strangely, they were Jewish.

The next day when the news came of the bombings, the merriment of the previous night was soon forgotten.

My family - and me - neighbours from hell! -

In my first marital home, a small semi, we lived next door on the driveway side to Gert (Gertrude) and Ernie (Ernest) During our time at this address we caused our poor long suffering older neighbours, several harassing incidents!

Pets or pests! - One day Gert came in complaining about our dog Bruno because he howled when we left him to go to work. We were talking by the side kitchen door. The doors of the two houses were opposite.

"I'm sorry, I just don't know what to do about it" I said feeling embarrassed.

"Well you've got to think of something!"

Whilst she was complaining about my dog, my cat, Whiskey, at that very moment was up to mischief! Unknown to both of us, Whiskey had entered her open kitchen door. When Gert went back into her house she let out a horrified scream and came rushing back to me as I was about to close my door behind me.

"Your cat has just stolen the fish for my husband's tea! And the cat has gone off through the window" – How calamitous! Fortunately for us she was fond of our cat and he was used to being welcomed in their house.

They were good neighbours but she used to amuse us in the way she referred to her husband, "My 'usband, wot's the manager of the works!"

In fact he worked in a draughtsman's office. It was a good job but the 'manager' title was complementary fantasy. Gert would get some word pronunciations wrong – for superfluous she would say 'super-fluous.'

(This particular comical error became entrenched in Geoff's mind to become part of his vocabulary … he will pronounce it this way, embarrassingly at times!)

Neighbours from hell - continued -

The woeful washing machine -My neighbour had a single chamber washing machine, a good model for that period. It was mobile on casters to enable it to be moved to be emptied outside in a drain at the side the house. There was only a single vehicle width between our houses that I used regularly to run my car to our garage. The neighbours did not have a car.

One day I went into the garage and reversed to go out to work. My heart leapt as I heard this ominous clank as I collided with something. I jumped out of the car and found Gert's washing machine leaning at an ominous angle on the boot of my precious M.G. TD sports car, my pride and joy.

Fortunately the washer escaped being mangled as it had managed to move along on two castors. A shocked Gert came running out of her kitchen,

"What have you done to my washer?!"

Fortunately, though a little scratched, it was still OK.

Neighbours from hell - Part three*!* -

The tale of the squashed bucket! - Reversing out of my garage once again, having walked up a clear drive, I again heard the ominous sound of collision, "Now what!" I breathed to myself wearily. Gingerly, I inspected the scene and discovered a distorted galvanized bucket jammed under the car bumper. Out runs Gert again, all agitated,

"Oh… *oh! Now*, you've flattened my bucket!"

Happily she was satisfied with my bucket -straightening skills. The observation of panel - beating techniques in the car trade certainly helped!

When my wife came home that day I said to her,

"I was reversing out of the garage ... and ... guess what?" -

"Oh no! Don't tell me! Not again!"

I was baffled how Gert managed to leave things out just after I had gone into the garage that had no doors, with the obvious intention of reversing the car down the drive. Only minutes of time were involved. I have had an aversion to shared drives ever since!

Neighbours from hell - part four!

A whitewash! - One day I came out of the front door, and looking up and down the avenue saw Ernie my neighbour up a pair of steps just inside his door- less porch which protected the front door. In one hand was a two-pint tin of white gloss paint, in the other the brush for the steps had no platform on which to place tools.

In breezy manner I called out, "Hi ya Ernie!"

Startled, he wobbled and dropped, not just the brush, but also the tin of paint! It fell in such a way on its bottom edge that the impact jettisoned out most of the paint in a remarkable fountain like manner! - It went everywhere! - All over the inside of the porch, the path, the glass of the half-glazed front door, some of the red brickwork, the floor, and naturally...Ernie!

"Why did you speak to me just then! ... Didn't you see ...?"

"I'm sorry, ah ... I didn't realise ...oh!"

I helped him clear up the mess, with *my* turpentine (Geoff being a generous guy!…?). The tedious job took an age.

They must have been a good-humoured saintly couple to have remained so patient and amiable with us, which they did! Probably they made allowances because we were newly weds and they were mature.

Neighbours from hell - part five!

A visit from a trowel - wielding 'angel' -

Our houses were brick-built with low brick front walls and timber personal gates. They were not built with cars in mind, so to make driving in possible I removed the small gate and some of my front wall and as there was a step down on to the path I built up a ramp.

I worked long hours at that time so I did not rush to tidy up the jagged bricks at the end of the now shortened front wall.

I came home from work in the car as normal one evening and as I approached my home I instinctively halted because I noticed something different about our gateway. I got out of the car to see what it was about.

Surprise, surprise! I saw that the brickwork that needed doing had been completed! The wall edge had been straightened and tidied and was finished off nicely with a gate post cap

I thought, 'My wife must have got someone in as a surprise, to save me the bother.'

As I stood there scratching my head, baffled, my neighbour Gert came strutting out in some obvious annoyance.

"They've come and done your gate but we have been on to the landlord for months to tidy up ours. How come you get yours done when you are *buying your House*?"

I was baffled, "I've no idea!"

Most of the houses were still owned by the same builder/landlord; presumably the man doing the job assumed that ours was still rented. As it was his mistake a bill never arrived! It was some months later that my neighbour's front wall and gate were fixed!

At that time we were planning to move to a shop in Newport, Ernie with a twinkle in his eye said,

"I dare say our lives are going to be a lot more humdrum when you've gone. I guess we'll be missing you and your disasters!"

The roar and charge of the Jaguar! -

I was visiting a garage in Cardiff S Wales with a view to buying a dark blue Humber Super Snipe car.

I was talking with the owner when a beautiful gleaming silver grey Jaguar 2.8 saloon car, the latest model, drove in at speed. We watched with mild concern.

The forecourt was square with the raised 'pump island' placed centrally and at right angles to the road. Instead of the owner alighting to use a petrol pump, the car, again at speed, immediately reversed and disappeared turning right on to the road from whence it came. Decidedly odd!

After a short time the car returned, again much too fast!

We both instinctively stepped back in stunned astonishment as the Jaguar mounted the island and ploughed through the pumps and accessories; in seconds demolished the lot!

- All the pumps (about three) were levelled and parts of the casing were propelled in all directions - oilcans bounced noisily and scattered everywhere!

The bewildered owner approached the driver who red-faced was grappling with the gearbox, engine still racing. The owner exploded -

"You stupid idiot! (or words to that effect!) In one sweep you've put me out of business!"

The explanation was that the driver, a mature man, had just purchased the automatic car from Howell's Show room just down the road. Obviously he had not received sufficient instruction in the handling of an automatic gearbox.

Fortunately there was little damage to the car …lucky him!

Sickly sweet

It was around 1954 a time of serious food rationing when I went on two weeks touring holiday mostly around Cornwall with my first wife and a couple of new friends met early in the holiday. We visited several Guesthouses and generally the hospitality was warm and generous – with the exception of one! The food portions were mean and unsatisfying. All four of us felt cheated. With a token gesture of complaint, after breakfast I emptied the remaining sugar from the sugar bowl into my trouser pocket to the accompaniment of 'naughty boy' giggles from my friends. The sugar would be handy to sweeten the flask tea on our travels that day. Having already paid we swiftly returned to our rooms to pack up and leave by creeping stealthily down the stairs.

However, as we crossed the hall, my friend Ken became aware of a crunching sound underfoot - it was the sugar! Looking round and up the stairs we spotted a tell- tale trail of sugar leaked from my trouser pocket! We increased our speed of exit and fortunately for us we were not apprehended.

(Comment by the author - "Granulated sugar in a trouser pocket! Humph! How daft, they deserved to get caught")

~

Reflecting on God's gift of humour –

Our little dog Rikky gazes at us in stupefaction tinged with alarm when Geoff and I - sometimes with others - howl and rock with laughter. But God blessed our species with the sense of humour because he knew that *we seriously* needed it! It is invaluable in helping us to keep sane when life gets crazy and mind-boggling!

The best form of humour is the ability to laugh at oneself – it is not available to the proud and haughty!

~

CHAPTER ELEVEN

The World Within A World

The irrefutable school of experience –

From what we have learned down the years from our own personal experiences, and those of many others, Geoff and I conclude that some people have a more inbuilt or natural gift than average of sensing *the world within a world;* this is true of most young children who for instance seem to easily pick up a belief in the God who cannot be seen or touched.

The parallel universe is a name that has been given to the unseen world that is interwoven so closely and mysteriously with our physical world. The psychic and/or spiritual sense of these unseen realities has been called the sixth sense or the third eye. It is a somewhat elusive region that in the main eludes convincing scientific investigation. There are reports of ghosts or other spiritual entities being caught on photographic film, sometimes accidentally.

The main religions of the world are aware of this unseen reality or *other world,* and base their beliefs on how these realities are perceived, whether mentally, logically, by dreams and visions or by inner perception. To people of faith it is *logical* to believe in a creator God, *not* illogical. Mankind on the whole senses this realm of being and individuals have experienced it within the soul or spirit - *the world within.* Confusion arises because there are so many different interpretations on what these perceptions signify.

Geoff became aware at six years old that he had this *otherworld* sense.

But as in the physical realm we experience the opposites of darkness and light, cold and hot, so in the *otherworld* realm we experience darkness and light, the evil and the good. It makes sense to pursue the good experiences of light that are warming and helpful rather than chilling and blood-curdling.

Those who become involved in the sinister, the macabre and the violent sooner or later are seriously harmed, psychologically or spiritually. Some become obsessed by evil urges to cause fear and even to torture and kill. Fears and nightmares haunt some.

Hallowe'en once a Christian festival of Hope celebrating the passage of saints into heaven has become distorted to a 'celebration' of blackness, horror and death by tricks, masks, broomsticks, images of horrific figures and so-on - designed to frighten and stir up fears, which may be hidden by nervous giggles. - In reality it is *partying* with emblems of the dark side of life. It may, *or may not*, be subtle but it is a form of abuse. It is a potentially long-lasting damaging experience for the young and vulnerable who can become haunted by fearful imaginings especially in the dark and in bed. Both of us as youngsters have experienced something of that fear reaction after seeing sad and frightening films.

~

It is known that young people in the years of puberty can generate poltergeist activity especially if the young person in question is going through a particularly turbulent time. We accept that a form of energy of *another world* kind can be produced in this sort of situation and seemed a reasonable explanation for what happened on the following occasion

~

A supernatural light -

For a couple of years we fostered a girl, she was in her early teens. She had been raised in Children's Homes and had suffered a difficult family background. She was a very angry, confused girl with a very low self-image although in fact she had a lot going for her. She probably did not realise until the end of her stay with us that we loved her.

For some months after she came to us she would talk for hours about her distressing memories.

One summer evening the three of us were relaxing in our sitting room. Our girl was talking when something strange occurred.

At either side of our fireplace were twin wall lights. They were switched off but they began to glow, the light strengthening, then fading. The episode took seconds but Geoff saw it all, our foster daughter saw most of it and I think I caught the fading of the light... Before this event Geoff had shivered with a sudden momentary coldness.

The rustle of ghostly skirts! -

Geoff had mentioned to a woman that he met at work that he was sensitive to atmosphere - she and her husband were considering buying an old large Jacobean house in grounds situated centrally in the attractive old historic village of Caerleon which is situated two miles from Newport Gwent/Monmouthshire It is sited on the then trading river Usk.

Caerleon still has the remains of the Roman Fortress of Isca amphitheatre and Roman baths and other remains. There is also a Museum - all of which is an attraction for tourists.

He arranged to make a visit with the couple and their teenage son and daughter.

He wandered around on his own. He felt a peace in the garden; it had a lovely old oak tree towards the rear, as well as other plants and shrubs.

Then he went into the house into the spacious carpeted hall from which ascended a lovely sweeping stairway to a wide landing, all in a lovely carved wood (probably mahogany).

He still felt peacefulness inside the house. The couple and children were far away in another part of the large house.

He was about halfway up the carpeted stairs, in fact had one foot touching the next step when he heard girlish chuckles followed by the distinctive swish of long skirts!

Then he heard a definite "Shushsh!"

The atmosphere was still peaceful; there was no sense of anything sinister or sad.

He found the family and related what he had 'heard'. He was then told that the house had been a private finishing school for genteel young ladies!

The couple was impressed with the house but chose not to buy because of repair and maintenance costs.

Obviously Geoff had somehow been given a peek into the past when the governess (or teachers) would be controlling natural youthful exuberance as the girls bounded noisily down the stairs.

Geoff has developed no set theory about what happens at these times but it is as though time merges - present with past.

A Heavenly Halo of Light -

Mary, my sister, just aged 60, was rushed to hospital after collapsing - she had been putting on weight. She was found to have advanced ovarian cancer so it required a massive operation - the weight was a fluid build up that was drained off - 7.5 litres in fact.

Many people loved her and prayed for her and many believed that it was because of this support that she recovered well from the operation, and remarkable quickly.

Geoff and I visited together about two days after the op. As we entered the small ward we saw her immediately as her bed was almost opposite to where we entered. She was sitting up in bed, looking lovely and smiling. Geoff halted for a moment in wonder. He saw around Mary a beautiful glowing light! He knew that she was wrapped in God's loving Care.

Overawed he said to her, "You are looking lovely Mary!"

She smiled serenely, "It is all the love and prayers that I am receiving!"

Interest in healing -

At one point Geoff became interested in the healing gift.

To a degree we all possess this as we demonstrate our love and concern for others, especially our children. We can all help others with a soothing word, a touch of the hand, a hug etc. A Mother says to her a young child who has fallen and hurt his knee, "Let me kiss it better!" She does so and often straightaway the child stops yelling and runs off to play.

If we programmed a high-tech robot to look human and do the same comforting gestures, it would fail! Geoff found that he had the ability to comfort animals. Even our dog (bitch) seemed to benefit from Geoff's touch, soothing the pain of minor injuries and after an operation done by the vet.

Elusive Mysteries of healing -

After a rapid convalescent period Mary enjoyed at least six months of a very active life.

"I've not felt so well for years!" She beamed.

But sadly, she was very ill again about a year after the op. She started suffering pain in the left side of her abdomen; for that reason we stayed a while with Mary and Maurice in the early spring of 1988. One lovely spring morning into the garden she took out her recliner to bask in the sun. She asked Geoff to place 'healing' hands on her, because he had discussed with her his presumed gift.

Placing his hands, he sensed the heat of her body on the one side and a natural coolness on the other. We know that some diseases cause heat and burning in the tissues so there was nothing strange about that; however, when he focused on healing he felt that it was not right, he felt an opposing power, and so stopped his efforts.

Geoff said, "There is a greater Power at work here, I can't do it."

Since then he and I have pondered a great deal about this to understand what it meant, what was going on.

A clue is that my sister was a committed Christian, she had accepted the living Jesus into her heart and life. She had been a missionary for around 14years and a preacher in local Churches for many years. Geoff had not committed his life to God through Christ. Therefore the two, although on good terms were not of the same spirit; it seemed that there was kind of clash in the realm of spirit.

Or, maybe God had a much higher spiritual purpose in this illness that we mere humans cannot possibly understand or presume.

Terminal cancer –

Mary did not survive the second attack. She knew in her heart that it was not of God, but matured Faith knows that nothing is beyond his creative loving purposes - even cancer. There are destructive powers at work in this world that are not always physical in nature, but Mary knew the reality of Divine Love, giving her patience, comfort, and a future Hope.

Mary never lost her inner peace, despite those terrible last few months. Some who came to her home in the last few weeks of her life commented on the feeling of peace there. The Peace that was a Gift to her by her faith was of that other *world within. The Light and Hope* of the other world was in her heart.

A soul's flight -

Geoff had yet another spiritual experience concerning Mary -We were sitting quietly at her home with her husband on the second or third day following her death when Geoff suddenly burst into tears for a brief moment.

"What is it?" I asked.

"I have just sensed her spirit depart! ... She is gone!"

We had yet more to learn about *a world within a world*

A Visitation from the Dark Side -

We had moved house to Yorkshire to be nearer my aging parents and two sisters. It was disastrous. Mostly everything about our lives did not work out and the stress caused both of us ill health. We needed to move again but had no idea where we should go. We had become confused and considerably distressed for we had left a good life behind in South Wales.

Curiosity is a natural human inclination but it can lead us into deep waters ...I had read that you could 'ask questions' of a pendulum. This is a weight hung on a piece of string. Our aim was to receive guidance for our next house move. As I had lost my inner Peace prayer seemed not to be working for me. We were about to experience something new, to us, of that other world within our world. It was so shocking that we must warn others of the dangers that we cannot know by the five natural senses.

~

Ministers of religion report that people come to them on the point of insanity as a result of becoming involved in the occult dark powers, these victims need special prayers, often for over a period of time.

It so easy to believe, like so many do, that all mysterious powers and energies are part of the natural Order, if a puzzling part of life. We were to dramatically discover that not all these powers or energies are operating for our lasting good - sometimes involvement is very dangerous spawning suicidal thoughts -even homicide!

~

Geoff narrates the following:

A black apparition -

There was a street lamp giving amber light only several feet away from our large bedroom window situated alongside Dorothy. Filtering through our curtains it created a subdued glow in the bedroom.

One night, I was awakened in fear soon after midnight. I was being pinned down by an invisible force. There was a pressure on my chest, I found difficulty in breathing and could not move a muscle. I was terrified and filled with foreboding, and fully awake to boot!

I noticed a movement to my left by the door that was adjacent to the bed head. - A short dark figure was entering the room and it moved to the foot of the bed, I saw it very clearly. It was no dream. Vaguely, it resembled an upturned black shuttlecock. There was a head shape but no features. The material was black. There was a cloak over the head to about the waist area where it seemed to fall in folds. The skirt was also fluted and reached the floor. I called out to Dorothy, but to my horror, I produced no sound. I felt terrifyingly powerless.

Dorothy slept on.

The apparition spoke -

"Upon thy death, thy soul shall be mine!" And then it silently glided back to the door and away.

It seemed like minutes - though probably it was seconds - before the pressure left my chest and I was able to move and rouse Dorothy. She knew nothing about what had happened!

Discussing it the next morning, my wife and I realized that the event had been a grave warning to us. I felt seriously shaken and knew then in my heart that we had been dabbling with powers that are dangerous to mental and spiritual health.

I had glimpsed and experienced for myself *the dark side of that world within a world*

Personal Discoveries -

This was the first time we had discovered at first hand for ourselves, that there are hostile forces at work - usually unseen - *within our world.* From that time both of us have strictly avoided any activity that is, or even seems, occult in nature for such activity is like stepping on to a slide whose downward slope may well be too subtle to be noticed at first, but is likely to grow steeper and yet more addictive, the more one dabbles in these occult (hidden) things..

Since this episode we have read accounts in books and articles, of people who have been held down by a sinister and invisible force.

Children can be affected and may show symptoms that appear like an epileptic fit. Often the house where they are staying or living is haunted or darkly affected by some dreadful event in the past, which leaves a form of spiritual contamination in the house. Some Churches, especially Anglican and Roman Catholic, can organise a special rite or service of prayers in such a property to 'cleanse' it.

Occult means 'hidden'.

Who in their right mind would venture in and explore a new and unlit region without guidance, without light? Sadly, very many do.

Ghosts –

In the chapter - 'The Strange *Other World*' two ghost stories and other super natural events are recounted.

CHAPTER TWELVE

THE DAY WHEN GOD SHOWED UP

Geoff narrates: -

AN ENCOUNTER WITH THE LIGHT SIDE OF THE WORLD WITHIN A WORLD

Through the years, it seemed that Dorothy and I were given a strong awareness that there is much more to life than the physical world and even God - whatever one's personal image or view of God might be.

~

In Western Culture any belief in unseen beings or powers such as demons and angels has been classed as superstition which education could be trusted to eradicate! The fact is that there are people who know first hand the truth about dark, destructive, unseen spiritual powers. People who have been brought up in cultures where Satanism, voodoo and other evil practices are rife have suffered the murderous violence that curses the individual and society as a direct result of these dark activities. We see it in the world today - societies being ravaged by a violence that feeds itself.

When the teaching of the so called Enlightenment was spread around - coming from Germany - exalting intellect and reason, this biased teaching numbed those delicate spiritual senses and discernment with which mankind was and is endowed albeit in varying degrees.

The miracles of the Bible were explained in practical or psychological terms by the mis-named *enlightenment*.

~

From childhood I have been convinced of God with a faith that would encourage others to go to Church to find faith but did not see the need to go myself because I was already a firm believer from the age of six.

I imagined that I had it all, more or less. What woeful ignorance! I did attend a few services in traditional Christian Churches over the years but found neither little benefit nor the enlightenment that I sought

In the early nineties Dorothy and I felt that we had to change house and location although at the time we were living happily in beautiful North Wales a few miles into the country from Caernarfon. In September 1992 we moved to St Martin's, a North Shropshire village; it brought us close to the canal system for narrow boat cruising, which was a hobby of ours. Later we believed that God had prompted us to make this move, and he managed the details of our house buying progress because a whole new chapter in life was soon to open for us both in our new location.

Within a few months we went to four specially planned and devised weekly meetings in a couple's house. It was in the Lent, pre-Easter period, 1993. I was impressed by the care and loving concern of the couple that was leading the meetings.

We were looking at some of the basic teachings of Jesus Christ. There were points and queries for discussion. I was then 66years old. I was congratulated on what I had remembered of the Bible Stories from my school days. I never went to Sunday school.

Being congratulated helped me feel an accepted member of the group. The real faith and enthusiasm of the leading couple and others in the group of around of 12 people impressed me. This was the first time that I had felt a spark of interest in organised Christianity.

The week following the four weekly house meetings was Holy Week. On the Tuesday evening, Dorothy went to a meeting at the Church - I stayed at home.

Dorothy arrived home a little later than normal because of interesting discussions at the meeting. I had started to feel quite ill through the evening with something akin to 'flu and sat in a chair waiting for Dorothy to come home before attempting to prepare for bed. Dorothy tells me that when she arrived home I practically fell on her in the hall in a distressed state, I was aching dreadfully in my arms and legs, and also I had a burning sensation developing in my throat and chest. But it seemed strangely different from anything that I had suffered before. Dorothy, a trained nurse, could not identify it as a known illness.

THE VISION

I went to bed that evening and continued to suffer into the second day. Normal domestic medication did little to relieve the condition. Then something incredibly dramatic happened to me around 4pm (April 7th 1993)

Inspiration from The East -

I was looking at an Easter card from the leaders of the House meetings (now very dear friends) The card, instead of showing the usual Easter bunnies and eggs, said "Easter Blessings" The word

Easter shrunk down; I saw only 'East' and I was reminded that it was in the East where the first Easter took place - the crucifixion of Jesus and his miraculous rising from the state of death.

I started to ponder on the horrors of the unjust trial and crucifixion of Jesus of Nazareth. I knew the story from school teaching.

A strange illness -

Whatever I was suffering from came to its peak. I felt that I was at the end of my life. And then the reality of Jesus' agony came to me ... *vividly* - the trial - the sentence - the beatings - the crown of thorns and the nailing, I felt that my pains were a very small taste of this agony. I was also experiencing, to a small degree, something of the humiliation of Christ.

I lay in this painful state for a while ... then I became aware of something in the room that mysteriously developed into a form of Light. I knew, dramatically and vividly that this was Christ, the Divine, as I saw the folds of a robe, flowing down steps. I knew that I was in the Presence of **The Lord God**!

I was engulfed by a sense of unworthiness and knew *that I must radically change.*

In his love *The Heavenly Lord had come* to transform me. And *I yielded to it.*

A soft brightness developed and settled completely over me like a healing coverlet - It was roughly the length and width of my body and I had the sensation of being cocooned in incredible Love! - The trouble in my soul, the pain in my hands, arms, legs and feet and the tunnel of fire in my throat, were taken away.

Beautiful Light and Love were soothing away all my suffering, cooling my feverish body and more wonderfully, washing me clean inside, producing in me a glorious state of Perfect Peace. I was a man re-created, made over, renewed!

The experience was not of this world, but truly, of heaven - *A world within a world*! - Heaven on earth!

I can find no words to begin to describe the wonder - the magnificence, of it. I thought that I was going through a very blessed death experience and I totally gave myself over to it.

Later, I understood it to be a baptism in the Holy Spirit of Jehovah God - a personal Pentecost, well-known in spiritually alive Christian circles. It happened to the first Christians soon after the resurrected Jesus was seen to rise up into the clouds and beyond to join his heavenly father.

I bathed in this Holy Presence -

A Perfect Peace seemed to permeate my being for what seemed to be an age. All my cares and guilt vanished.

The cake -To my left I became aware of a cake displayed on a stand. I reached out to it but it moved out of reach by a mechanical system of bolts and arms which were distinct in detail. My focus was then drawn to the right.

The black boxes - I saw a hanging black sheet with large black boxes in each corner. I knew that these represented my many sins. I had a desperate urgency to destroy them. I vigorously pulled them down and crammed them into a dark pit at my feet - the darkness was suddenly transformed!

The pit became infused with light!

I felt a joyous lightening in my spirit. I knew that by the Power of Grace and Divine Love, my sins, the dark side of my nature, by way of silent repentance, had been dealt with. I was completely forgiven!

I knew in my heart that though I was still a long way off perfection, amazingly I was now acceptable in God's sight. My worst sins were meanness and an unforgiving, revengeful spirit - a hard heart - resulting in the desire for revenge on those who upset me. I would wish evil and misfortune on people I resented who had hurt or harmed me.

A mighty miracle had occurred. I subsequently found that these evil desires had been removed.

It was like a surgical procedure on my very soul!

Of course, other faults remained that still needed attention but the worst had been removed!

But the Vision continued -

The cake reappeared; this time it had been half consumed. I knew that it symbolised God's Blessing; I had just received a Feast of God's love symbolised by the missing half of the cake. The remainder of 'the cake of blessing' was to do with the future. And I had my part to play in this.

Then I became full of a joy of the spirit that I had never known before. I felt clean and light inside. How awesome! I had been wonderfully touched by Almighty God and just knew that this encounter had been made possible by what had been achieved on the cross at Calvary through the suffering of the God/man Jesus.

The historical Jesus of Nazareth, born a carpenter's son, two thousand years ago, suddenly became a living reality, for me, in the end of the twentieth century!

I now knew that he was not merely a character in a history book - he was now my Saviour and Master, living somehow on the inside of me. The Great Mystery of Grace.

Eureka! I had encountered a mysterious and miraculous *world ...within*! It was through the spiritual power of Jesus. He had saved me from the worst of myself and he would continue his character pruning work for the rest of my life! I have never felt more alive, before or since.

I felt that I would explode *with a new and Holy Joy*!

- And there was more...

God was not finished with me yet!

I felt myself picked up and transported away, body and soul so it felt, it was so real! But my body was left behind, as Dorothy who was with me throughout would confirm.

I found myself in the local Anglican Church - I had never worshipped there - God's purpose for me there was to rehearse my telling the people what God had done for me. And so I had a vision of the congregation and me standing before them to tell of my Heavenly Visitation. Then curiously, I was divided in two! One part of me was in a pew monitoring my 'performance'! - It had to be done properly you see!

In all this time I was aware that the altar was ablaze with a Brilliant Glory Light, and it was shining on to the faces of the people, who were aglow! Turning to the altar to worship my arms sprang into the air spontaneously for - The Presence of the Lord was so overpowering that I was bursting with awe and thankfulness...and the touch of Heaven!

The solemn Task -

I became keenly aware that a solemn task or mission had been given to me - To tell of this experience was only the beginning - I was to continue to spread the Truth of the Holy Bible and Jesus who enables one to experience God's free forgiving love, a Love which cannot be earned – only accepted.

Also I was to share 'the Words' - the messages and teaching that he chose to pour into my mind from time to time.

- *And there was still more!* -

I saw the local vicar/priest standing near me by the altar. Then I heard the first audible words of my experience-

"**I AM** says: This truly, truly, is a man of God."

Then I was instructed to place my hand over his head and bless him!... What! ... Me! ...What right did *I* have to do such a thing! Jim was indeed a dear, humble servant of Christ; but, to bless him, in front of the congregation?! ... It was a Divine command!

Tears of pure joy -

Finally I was back in bed - tears were pouring, not down my face, but spraying virtually, from the corner of my eyes!

Dorothy, who was quietly reading by my side, became aware of my weeping and new instinctively that God had been ministering to me or doing a special work in me - for she and other friends had been praying for me. She had wondered if my unusual illness had all been part of God's plan to get my attention, to soften me in order to enable me to receive His Grace! It does not happen to the self-sufficient.

~

In ancient times before the God of the Bible had given His name as Jehovah, He had called himself 'I AM' – a strange and unique verb tense to mean an ongoing endless past present and future status. Geoff had no knowledge of this.

God spoke to Geoff introducing himself by that ancient appellation: "I AM" - Names in Bible times were intended to be descriptive of that person or something about them. Jesus, in the New Testament, changed the name of his disciple Simon, to Peter 'the rock', because Jesus knew that he possessed Christ-based solid rock-like qualities.

Meditating on these parts of the Old Testament, one has the feeling that because God is the Source and Energy of All things, no name could suitably encapsulate the nature of his Being.

The greatest miracle of all -

There can be no greater or more glorious miracle on this earth than when God meets man, woman, or child - enfolding and embracing that one in a sense of Divine Love and Favour; Love in the Gift of free forgiveness and reconciliation. *It is a Gift,* **for it cannot be merited** and true conversion takes place! - At that point the spirit is awoken to the bliss of eternal realities of Spirit.

It is like receiving inner eyes and ears. The entire focus and priority in life is changed.

~

"Oh, Dot! I have had the most incredible experience! More real and ecstatic than anything that I have ever known or could possibly imagine!"

Dorothy stood up and started dancing up and down, arms waving in excitement,

"Does that mean that you have come to the Lord?"

"Yes! But... he came to me!" - HALLELUJAH! WHAT A SAVIOUR!

What a privilege! *But what an awesome responsibility.*

Subsequently -

I met with Jim the vicar at home to arrange to give my testimony, as God had instructed, to the local congregation. My excited zeal and godly mission was thwarted and distressed for the vicar wanted some time to elapse before I shared my vision. Understandably, no doubt, the delay was to test the authenticity of my experience and my response to it, and especially as I had no previous experience of Christianity or Church attendance. Furthermore, he had never met me before - except when we went to the pancake Race and the following meal, on the fun day, Shrove Tuesday!

Jim was embarrassed by his involvement in my experience; no doubt he felt that God had been too generous in his description of him! How remarkable that God has more faith in us that we have in ourselves!

But arrangements were made just a few weeks ahead for me share my wonderful story.

~

Reflections - Sadly, many today in our Western culture have ceased to expect mystical or visionary encounters with God. Some Christian groups believe that all supernatural things including spiritual gifts, stopped after the first apostles died. But in the history books of the Roman Catholic Church there are many accounts of miracles and *other world* mystical experiences. These experiences are normally attributed to individuals who have taken up the religious life, or those who have led particularly virtuous lives, or they are children.

Today, seemingly ordinary people can be miraculously blessed or chosen and empowered for a special task.

Agents for another world -

Aeronauts can be said to be ambassadors or agents for a world far away; a place that is inaccessible to the majority and we are all happy to accept their report with only a few being genuinely jealous of their opportunity. But when a visionary recounts their 'spiritual journey' they are frequently met with jealousy, scepticism or derision.

Geoff with deep sadness sometimes senses these negative responses when he relates his story.

But though imagination, even drugs, or desire to seek attention may sometimes motivate such stories, the Scriptures are full of accounts that involve the spiritual plane and they can serve as tutor and guide when weighing up the validity of recent similar accounts.

Yet these experiences *must not* be sought or some thing not of God could be experienced. People have come a cropper, some mentally ill, who have sought *other -world* experiences

But God from time to time chooses someone to be, as it were, an agent for the *otherworld* sphere. They become akin to journalists 'travelling' to that other world reality, to report back what they have seen, heard and felt, for the eternal benefit of the rest of us!

Passing an exam or studying theology is certainly not a requirement for being eligible for *a touch from God*, but a humble penitent attitude coupled with faith, is certainly a requirement. God often chooses very ordinary people for a special mission or purpose that can have a transforming effect on multitudes.

What a pity that a closed ear can deny one the joyful inspiration of the great 'news' that they, the visionaries bring 'back' - bringing exciting reports that this life is just a part or episode in the whole amazing scenario of Life - that earth-life is a flawed shadow image of a far more superior reality!

To listen with an eager open heart to the spiritual report of another can be life changing, life - enhancing!

GOD, FOR HIS OWN PURPOSES, CAN CHOOSE ANYONE TO REVEAL THE THINGS OF HEAVEN!

~

Geoff continues: -

Standing before the people -

Just before that particular morning service which was planned around my experience I was in a dreadful state of nerves. I was sweating and trembling and told Dorothy that I was not going to make it

"Yes you will!" she said... "Pray!"

So I simply asked the Lord to calm me down. The response was immediate! Suddenly the shaking stopped and I felt cool! All the symptoms of fear went! But before the start of the service Jim took me into the vestry for prayer. Then he handed me a slip of stiff paper on which was written a Bible quotation in bold red letters:

"FEAR NOT, FOR I HAVE REDEEMED YOU, I HAVE CALLED YOU BY NAME, YOU ARE MINE!" (Holy Bible Isaiah chapter 43 verses one.)

A thrill runs downs my spine These words were as if directly and personally spoken to me. They were like an arrow of light- and-warmth to my heart bringing a new tingling feeling of intimacy with *the-God-out-there* who had suddenly, become *the-God -in-here*! Somehow He was within me! It was a revelation - I now *knew* him as my Father, as Jesus did!

What an incredible WOW factor!!

And since the coming of the Holy Spirit to the first Christian believers, people throughout the earth and time have experienced this.

My spirit was now in communion with His spirit! What a Mystery! What a Miracle! Wonderful promises and reassurance in the Bible continue to thrill me!

The service was a beautiful and memorable experience. I told the story of my encounter with God, just as it was in my vision.

Several people were blessed, especially the younger and newer Christians. I have no doubt that some older members of the congregation were dubious and uneasy - and sadly, envy and disbelief can play a part in those who have had no special Godly experience.

My meeting with God gave me a love for the Scriptures that consequently I endeavour to read daily. I found a powerful, uplifting, inspiration in hymns, and especially in songs of adoration and worship. I also found that gathering informally with other believers of Jesus of like mind and heart became such a joy and blessing.

The non-organised Universal Church of Christ is a spiritual fellowship that crosses all the Christian denominations.

Roman Catholics and Protestants are meeting together all over the world, as it were to sit at Jesus' feet to connect with him in a real way and to get to know him more.

The riches and wisdom of all traditions can be learned and pooled into a rich mix. There are things to be learned also from people of other religions who also to some extent have grasped Universal Spiritual Truths. A great man of spiritual strength and peace was the celebrated Hindu Indian leader Gandhi, (1969 – 1948) who reflected on other beliefs, including Christianity. He was assassinated by a Hindu fanatic.

~

A delusional fantasy - Tragically, some people find it convenient, or logical, to believe that God is fantasy and a delusion, that this life is all there is

Amazing indeed, that inspired by this *Great Delusion* there are libraries and shelves all over the world full of books and works of art produced by adherents of the many religions on this earth.

The world is dotted with countless magnificent buildings of worship and beautiful religious statues... This is surely food for thought!

What a sadly cynical view of man's noble aspirations is the belief that all this labour and creativeness is based on an imaginary 'bubble' or sense of human insecurity and inadequacy.

Religious and spiritual people everywhere may get the details of the *other world* - including God - sadly or even *badly* wrong but the essential core belief or *sense* of a Supreme Being or Powers is basically the same.

~

Home At Last

If we confess our weakness and our need,
And own - our total strength falls short indeed,
And humbly bend in gratitude before God's chosen One,
Whose agony of body - soul, perfect salvation won
In shame and horror on that bloody tree,
Not just 'for all' - but for the one called - 'Me'

If we submit our wisdom flawed - our proud self-focused will
The King of glory will come in, our deepest need fulfil,
To satisfy the hunger of the soul,
In fellowship with God,
Life's Precious Goal.

CHAPTER THIRTEEN

THE AMAZING TRANSFORMATION

BECOMING A COMPLETELY DIFFERENT PERSON

In a nutshell Geoff's experience was an encounter with Divine Love, some of which was transmitted into his own heart

This visionary experience was the high point of his life. It started a relationship that is wonderful, enduring and very precious. Through the experience he discovered his true nature and the purpose for which he was born, namely to develop a *heavenly* relationship which will never cease and will develop beyond the grave.

Very many people in this world have made the same discovery but not often in such a non-disputable dramatic way! So *as one who knows*, Geoff feels compelled to share his revelation.

Geoff has had many interesting and challenging experiences in his life though his limited education narrowed his scope and earning ability. A minus is the lack of fulfilment in parenthood when children did not come. But regrets of what might have been exert no hold on Geoff. There are no regrets in his heart eating away at present possibilities of satisfaction because he has found the one thing that more than compensates for life's disappointments.

He has met a Person who has more than filled in the gaps where family or fortune could have been. That person is Jesus, now a spiritual Being, who has become the greatest living personality of all time in the ones who have found him. And he is the King of that *other* world as he has revealed himself to some. During his time on earth this king became a pauper and finally a condemned criminal suffering an horrific death as he paid the awesome price to be the Saviour of the world.

The riches and joys of the *other world* are *so much more* than compensation for failures and losses in this life. It is a meeting of spirit with Spirit that initiates radical change at the core of ones being. Priorities, perceptions and goals are turned around.

Having no children is a pity but Geoff does not feel that he has missed out on what **really** matters. I share in this perception.

Geoff speaks again –

My Damascus Road experience -

I have called my encounter with God my Damascus Road experience because of the similarities between my vision and the vision of St. Paul the Apostle. His story is told in the book of Acts (deeds) in the Bible. His name was Saul before his encounter with God but it was changed to Paul after his nature was radically changed when the Lord turned around the direction of his life. Similarly, the Lord clearly told me that he has named me 'Jethro' – a biblical name

Some people have had a mystical experience like Paul and myself; but most people have come to a living faith by responding to the gospel in the hearing or reading of it; or through the witness and testimony of believers. They have 'heard' God's welcoming voice - responding in faith and repentance. It is a step of faith into a whole new and wonderful life-giving and life-transforming experience. The sacrificial love of Jesus Christ is what melts the heart - the rejection and extreme suffering to which he submitted is so moving and humbling.

God, by way of a vision of Jesus, showed up for Saul/Paul when he was travelling on the road to Damascus. At that time, Saul was quite satisfied with his life and comfortable with his religion. He felt to have a good purpose in his mission of persecuting the new apostate religious group, the Christians. Like so many today he was not prepared to look further or probe more deeply into what motivated them... until God intervened!

Similarly, like Saul, I too was quite satisfied with my life as it was. Like so many I felt comfortable with my personal faith and believed that it was quite satisfactory; it was good enough - so I thought! Oh dear!

Wonderful changes happened -

Unasked, God touched me in transforming power, he changed my view of myself, others, God, and life... it is such a wonderful thing to receive an inner revelation of the perfection of God's Love and his desire to forgive us and embrace us. God has a huge heart; he loves every creature and wants to make us humans his children and to *treat* us as his children! He wants *us* to share *his* glory! What a thought!

He does not want us to try to struggle to be good before we dare expect his Love and favour; there was absolutely nothing saintly or altruistic about me! He will embrace us, as we are, providing that we are willing *to be* changed and redirected. Nor does he expect us to become perfect overnight!

He is patient and happy to forgive us if we say "Sorry" with genuine regret and real desire to be transformed, realising that we have lived our life *our* way, often being careless about others, and we have offended our conscience in various ways.

A change at Heart -

I had some very unpleasant characteristics before God changed me.

But he has softened my hard heart and though I still get impatient and annoyed with people it is not now spiked with malice or revenge. I am conscious of a love and concern for people that I did not have before.

I have come to know a sense of personal significance and planned place in this vast Universe.

These new convictions develop and strengthen as one walks the walk of faith and obedience and in fact are powered by the *world within* of which God can give us all an insight. Help is given by studying Scripture, meditation, prayer, praise and fellowship with other believers.

My universe was small and mostly self-centred.

This new song is my song: - Verses from Psalm 40

"He taught me to sing a new song,a song of
praise to our God.
Many who see this will take warning and will
put their trust in the Lord
In the assembly of your people Lord
I told the good news that you saved me
You know that I will never stop telling it!
I have not kept the news of salvation to myself."

The blessings following the Gift of the Holy Spirit that have come to me cannot be described adequately. So many spiritual blessings: - the Joy, glimpses of Glory - at special times experiencing His touch which transmits Peace and Power for healing There is an awareness and evidence that God, now my father, is steering me through this life and has kept me safe in hazardous situations.

Physical signs of God's Power - I am one of those who experience God in a physical way from time to time but never more powerfully than the first time he touched me and shook me up! These signs are not given to everyone.

At least twice I have nearly been knocked over by a sudden touch of God's Power, usually it happens in praise or prayer with other like-minded believers, many Christians have fallen over like this and then rested quietly, sometimes with a helper quietly praying on their behalf - this has been called 'resting in the Spirit' which is a form of healing. Some experience God like a mild electric shock. Some shake and this is how the original Quakers acquired their nickname – they shook when silently praying – seeking and to a degree finding - God.

Some have been spontaneously healed in Spiritually charged meetings. Some have been given the Gift of wisdom and supernormal knowledge.

A new delight is to make new friends of the faith in various places and from different ethnic groups, people who share and confirm my beliefs.

It was after the crucifixion and resurrection of Jesus that the Miracle-Gift of the Holy Spirit was given at the first Pentecost to indwell the believers who were waiting in faith for the promised Holy Spirit to come.

The Lamb's Book of Life - By the Grace of God and through his promises, I know with a deep seated assurance that my name, and Dorothy's name, is written in the Lamb's Book of Life - that record book in Heaven, and on the palm of God's Hand, as the Bible so poetically puts it! Oh, what intimacy is possible with the Creator of all things and Lord of all!

I have firmly locked Jesus into my heart - he has pride of place there for he suffered much for me and still suffers as he sees the weakness of faith and devotion in his people.

King Solomon in the Bible was granted special wisdom, but later he fell from favour as he compromised his beliefs and loyalty to God - which sadly is not an unfamiliar kind of story today. I pray that I will not stumble or wander away and lose what I have been freely given

Of course there are many unanswered and vexing questions. We are all distressed at the terrible suffering and injustice in the world and we become upset when some of our prayers seem to attract the "No!" Response!

But a stubborn need to know the answers to those vexing questions will act as a barrier to the development of intimacy with our heavenly Father.

However one day we shall understand these mysteries.

The discovery of a Gift and new understandings -

Some who have experienced an encounter with God find that they have been given a supernatural gift, usually called a 'Gift of the Spirit'. Soon after the Lord visited and touched me I discovered that I had been given Gifts of *discernment* and *prophecy,* the latter meaning 'inspired word' described in the next chapter. Roughly, discernment can be called the ability to detect between the genuine and the false. It is also the discerning of motives, as whether a preacher is a promoter of Truth or him/ her-self and their ideas and position.

I believe that the power of God is as real and involved with individuals and in human affairs as in the days of the Bible.

And there's more –

As one walks the *New Life* path – there are lovely times of answered prayer and great blessings, some miraculous, but there are the difficult, sad, puzzling and disappointing times. But meanwhile, the Word of God - the Scriptures, is my daily spiritual food. The Bible is the Living Word of God and it can move one to the core of one's being by its teaching of God's loving care and protection, his awesome promises, his Gift of a perfect Life to come - and his infinite patience with us his children

When I feel down there is always someone or something to lift my spirits again.

Grief –

However, there is a new kind of sharp grief – it is a heart pain for a suffering world that has lost its way and a grieving for all those in the world who have not yet discovered their true spiritual identity which is the potential of a warm relationship with a loving God who longs to be their Father, Saviour and friend.

CHAPTER FOURTEEN

THE GIFT

MANY SPECIAL GIFTS OF THE Spirit were given to the first body of Christian believers. These are different from the natural talents with which people are endowed. The Gift may be an enhancement of a natural talent or something extra of a supernatural or supernormal nature.

In recent times there has been a revival in these supernatural gifts.

The gift of prophecy is one such gift - it is the ability to receive a direct and spontaneous communication from heaven. It can be a creative or inspired idea or a warning - it can be a strong mental image or picture with symbolic meaning - it can be a short or very long message or communication based on Bible teaching or Bible truths.

Prophecy can be insight into or a warning of future events already spoken of or hinted at in Biblical Prophecy. In recent years God has given this Gift to many, especially recent Christians.

Generally, the recipient needs to be in prayer or sitting quietly in a state of relaxation or meditation. It can happen in a Church meeting or service, usually where the people are truly worshipping and expectant of a 'touch' from God.

It may happen at home in personal prayer. It can happen to a preacher seeking 'a word' from God when prayerfully studying and preparing an address. There is no straining mental effort.

For those with this gift it is not unusual to be awakened in the night hours to 'hear' words pouring into the mind. (Those with a special intercessory prayer gift may be awakened with the urge to pray for a certain person or situation because there is a particular need or danger, sometimes known to God alone at that time).

Geoff speaks of his discovery -

A little later, after my Godly encounter, I discovered that the Lord had given me what is known as a prophetic Gift.

The way the Gift works for me:

From time to time, usually when I'm in prayer, alone or in a prayer fellowship God pours a message into my mind. He has woken me up in the night or early morning on a few occasions.

At the beginning of my Christian experience, pictures with a meaning, like a parable in the Bible, often came into my mind, giving a message about my Church at the time.

I give some examples of these heavenly communications to my heart and mind: -

"**Malachi!"** On one occasion I was awoken with this word in my head. It meant nothing to me so I leisurely stretched, sat up and swung round to sit on the edge of the bed preparing to rise. Then again in my head I heard**, "Read Malachi!"**

God had spoken to me distinctly, twice. I had no knowledge what Malachi might be! It could have been a modern classic novel for all I knew. Dorothy explained that it was the last book in the

Old Testament of the Bible. Importantly, this book has strong teaching and warnings relevant to life today.

Some time later, just as clearly, on awaking, God said to me -

"**Read Habakkuk!**" Again I had to check out what this was for I had no knowledge of it - it is the fifth book from the end of the Old Testament. This book has similar warnings and teaching to Malachi.

Sentences sometimes came into my mind that are from Scripture-

"Your ways are not My ways" - this Dorothy recognised as being a phrase from the Book of Isaiah Chapter 55 verse 8.

I heard more words following on -

"I will take you to the pits of life and I will raise you to the heights of heaven - - what you do in between, I shall be watching!"

I understood this to mean that I would have hard and sorrowful experiences between the lovely blissful times of spiritual wonder and joy giving a foretaste of heaven. Times of trial are all part of The Plan to test and try us to see if we are candyfloss at heart or are becoming a people of substance - spiritual substance - ready for the next life!

Some messages that come are *too challenging* for the ears of those who see God as all-loving and all-embracing, a kind of sugar-daddy who somehow can turn a blind eye to life styles that the bible calls sin! But the Bible reminds us that he is a Holy and Righteous God who can and does burn with anger.

The narrow road to Life:

Another picture I saw was of a narrow road. It was strewn with rocks and potholes - at times it skirted a dangerous bank. I knew that these represented the distractions and temptations in life that can lead us into futile endeavours that do not feed the inner 'spirit - man'- do nothing to store up for us lasting treasures in heaven.

I saw people walking up this road weighed down with baggage. I knew that these loads represented the baggage of negative emotions and unnecessary goals like all-consuming ambition, and things like: -

guilt, resentment, anger, self-pity, remorse, self - condemnation, an unforgiving spirit and regrets. Also there are unhelpful memories that we may carry along with us. The Bible refers to these things as 'bondage'.

At the end of this path was a building; it had a name 'The Saloon of the Last Chance'

The meaning of the path -

The path was the way of truth and love, the way of life to which Jesus referred. He said that it had a small gate and the path or road from it was narrow. He warned that few find it. It can also be called the path of faith and obedience. Jesus taught that the way to destruction was broad. The life lived for Love of God and humanity also follows a strict moral code.

The 'Saloon' message means that there is a time when the good way of faith, integrity and love can be found, but if conscience is repeatedly ignored the heart will become hard when conscience will no longer be heard. Prior to irreparable damaged there will be a 'last chance' The consequence of hard-heartedly ignoring the warnings of conscience leads to a dreadful future of an eternity in the hell of regret and self-condemnation - and whatever else there is - on the plane of the dark side of a future world. This law of *cause and effect* is known by some Faiths as the Law of Karma. It is has similarities to the Bible principle that teaches that we shall reap what we sow. We are looking at unchangeable spiritual principles and forces operating in this world.

Now is the time -

A time limit is an unacceptable concept to many, and also to some people with faith, but the warning about a time limit was clearly give in this picture –

One of the first pictures that I had was the image of a watch - the hands were almost on the midnight hour, then it disintegrated! This was a warning again that we are given a certain time to get our lives on the right track. If we fail to take our opportunity, or keep ignoring conscience, our chance is gone and then Hope is lost forever. I had a *strong* sense of warning with this clock image.

~

The elevating Christ Spirit is it at work throughout the world, whether we come to realise this or not, seeking to reach the human heart whatever our religion, race or time span, to lift us on to the higher plane – on to the True path based on love expressed in all the spheres of life's relationships and towards humanity in general. And even - perhaps especially, in the midst of unjust and evil situations motivated by hate and greed. For the heart of God is love.

~

The ascent -

Another picture that I was given showed a tree with many people climbing it. There were people stranded on the top branches, some were falling off – after the effort of the climb they discovered that there was nowhere to go, the climb had been wasted effort.

There were labels attached to the tree -*ambition - fame - power - wealth.*

The lesson was that these raw, egoistic ambitions achieve nothing for the eternal state of the soul/spirit. They are dead end pursuits.

Adjacent to the tree was a picture of two radiantly happy people being transported in a chariot. It was climbing steeply upwards into the sky, pulled by angels and winged white horses. I had the impression of a beautiful city, way up heavenwards.

The people in the chariot were joyously waving a free pass in their hands!

I knew that the picture meant that the way to true salvation and fulfilment is by faith in the life and sacrifice of Christ on the cross and following his way of love and sacrifice.

Riches and fame are not wrong in themselves but carry a weight of extra responsibilities and stress; also they stir up envy from covetous people who may pose, falsely, as friends. We leave all these goods and acquisitions behind and the Wills of the deceased often generate bad feeling.

Though the way we live is important, for our deeds are recorded in heaven, these are not enough. The 'pass' or ticket to Glory, or heaven, is free! It is by Grace! *It cannot be earned*! This God-designed system is set to avoid boasting - a symptom of the serious sin of human pride.

The Divine Purpose of the Prophetic Gift -

God does not want us to be ignorant of main developments in the future. He also teaches that faith in Him and obedience to Godly laws will auger well for the future. Some future calamities are inevitable but some can be averted. Mankind brings upon himself/herself disasters that are avoidable. We learn that people who live near powerful volcanoes do not always heed the warnings of those who watch the signs. Whatever the reasons for it there are global climate changes and it is happening faster than many scientists have guessed.

God has tried to tell us that a day of reckoning is coming for us all. Some people think that their disbelief will somehow keep them safe! There are going to be many deeply shocked and scared people who have chosen to keep their heads in the sand!

Advice and serious Warnings of Catastrophic Things To Come

(Some already have happened since this warning)

Fire and Hatred -

Not long before the world suffered devastating fires in places around Indonesia and elsewhere due to drought and abnormal winds, I received this message on October 28th 1997: -

"Reach out your hands together with your hearts, seek my protection, surround yourselves completely with My Truth, it is to be found through my words. Read the truth (Scripture), the answers are there for you, live this Truth, the time is NOW!

"Each of you must heed My Words, protect and obey The Word; believe, and be ready to stand firm. My

Strength is in you my children, stay together more and more. The trials and tribulations are soon to be confronted - (confirming Bible Prophecy) fire and hatred will abound throughout your earth.

"Abide in my Words, feel the pressures and resist ALL you know to be wrong. I have spoken to many a listening ear, heed their warnings.

"Praise the Lord Jesus for your continuing salvation".

Significantly, this message was given before 'the preachers of hate' became a threat to society.

The curse of the foot and mouth disease:

In 2001 when farming was hit by this terrible disease I received this message:

"Open the gates and allow all my creatures the freedom of the lands that they share with all my creation. No more will I tolerate them being used for man's greed and gluttony"

There was also a serious outbreak of disease amongst intensively reared hens in the 1980's, many of us fearfully remember. Since then there have been outbreaks and scares of disease amongst animals and fowl, domestic and wild

Let the Animals Run Free

The nation is reeling with the plague of 'foot & mouth'.
This fatal curse is spreading wide, across and North and South.
But let us not be foolish here to think it's plain bad luck,
For round us is the evidence, the reasons, if we look.
It's not the wheel-of-fortune's hand that dealt this fateful blow,
Imperative it is, again, we go with Nature's Flow.

The steady yield from farming now from cattle, pig and sheep
Is shattered by Catastrophe "What next?" the farmers weep.
But, there's a pattern in this life - the Law of Cause/Effect,
Disaster comes to human kind who cannot this detect;
For those with common sense - they see and know this problem clear.

We can't exploit dumb animals to cause them pain and fear.

The pain of journeys far and wide, in heat, cold, traffic's fume
Fear-racked by thirst, gasping for air crushed upright with no room;
Then at the end of that dread trip, exhausted stressed and wan,
To death into the abattoir, they're pushed and whacked - to run..
The creatures whose very nature is to burrow and to dig,
Are penned in wire cages - no respite for the humble pig.

What hypocrisy for a generation that loves to shout its 'rights'
When deliberate abuse of animals has now reached such shameful heights;
We cannot blame the farmer, bound in the Economy Trap,
The Icons of wealth - Big Business Groups have pinned us in their lap.
When farmers are selling their meat for a song,
It is dear in big markets - Just isn't that wrong?

They shut down the local slaughter house, they reckoned it did not pay,
Instead the stock pays a terrible price, in suffering haulaged away.
It's time to get together now, to make a common stand,
Unnatural ways are ruining us, dishonouring our good Land.
PLEASE! Ministers in government, is profit all you care?
Relieve the evil suffering our animals now bear."

And all of us must think again, our spending styles debunk,
Invest in food the base of life, less on harmful useless junk!
For if we try to change the Laws that govern this fair Earth,
To plague and pestilences shall the Human Race give birth.
Fling wide the gates, let stock roam free or sickness will get worse
Sure, the Power that drives the Universe will pour on us Grief and Curse!

The New Creation -

One morning in March 2005 I was prayerfully resting when the following words came into my mind from God. It was a compelling experience and caused me to weep.

The quote is a part of a long passage; it is addressed to obedient believers –

"In the New creation He (Jesus) will be your mighty Saviour and you will know by the power of his love that you will be part of the New World that will never be destroyed by disobedience, neither by man, nor by darkness and evil."

The same teaching can be found in Revelation Chapter 2: 25-29 & Chapter 3: 8-12

Chapter 22:20 -"Even so, come. Lord Jesus." And so let it be

CHAPTER FIFTEEN

The Argument For Future Hope

SUMMING UP TOGETHER – GEOFF AND DOROTHY

Believers know in their hearts that despite evidence to the contrary there is a Mighty Unseen Hand on the rudder of this flawed world as it tosses on the tumultuous seas of man-made catastrophes and wild nature. That hand is there to reach out and save from final destruction the individual who admits his/her need and serious character imperfection and calls out for help.

People of faith normally need a doctrine or theory to underpin their beliefs. Faith may be simple or something dynamic that has been triggered unexpectedly by the powerful hand of God projecting the recipient spinning into the orbit of a new and wonderful world.

However, evil poses a vexed question; fanaticism is the greatest plague of this world – past and present. Mainly it comes in one of two guises – politics or religion. This evil is the most deadly when the two are mixed.

A common explanation for the work of evil in the world is that humans had to be given free choice between good and evil. We were made in God's 'image and likeness' (Genesis chap 1 verse 26) meaning that we were made as spirit beings, restricted for a time in a body, but not robots. The Divine intention was for us be in close relationship with God, the Supreme Spirit Being, to share his Glory and magnificent Heavenly Kingdom. Serious choice is necessary to come into an intimate relationship with that Supreme Being, and there are conditions.

The rampages of evil in the world, the injustices, the continual suffering and the agonies and helplessness of its victims trouble believers of all faiths and unbelievers alike. But the very preciousness of life and consciousness *must* be worth the price of pain in all its forms - Jesus thought so, he faced unimaginable agony and humiliation to achieve the purpose for which he came to earth.

Simply put, his purpose was to heal the breach between God and humanity.

Struggling with temptation –

Jesus himself quoted the inspired Scriptures of old to help him stay on the higher path, to remind him of the spiritual road that is in stark contrast with natural human wisdom and desires. He fought the temptations of manipulative power, magic, celebrity status, wealth and fame by *preaching to himself,* as well as Satan, the wisdom of scripture. He urges us to do likewise. We read the account in Luke's record in chapter 4 of his gospel.

Jesus was given authority and power by God because he was the prophesied Christ who was to suffer on behalf of mankind; though an innocent man he was cruelly executed and then rose from the dead on the third day. Scriptures teach us that Jesus was predestined to be a ransom sacrifice to buy us back from a spiritually-lost state.

We are destined to die both physically and spiritually because we became estranged from God but Jesus was destined to die in our place that we might be transformed and given again the gift of unending life.

☺ What an amazing Master to follow, he has *so much* to offer

☺ What a joy and a privilege it is to be a believer in and follower of Jesus.

Spiritual cleansing -

Divinely happy are those, throughout the globe, who are already benefiting from this special kind of spiritual healing that is available through the power of the active living spirit of Jesus in the world, able to dwell in the human heart, to impart a 'knowing' that has been the assurance and the drive of martyrs to courageously accept cruel persecution and tortured death. (The proof of the pudding is in the eating).

Fantasy Or Fact

The atheist says –"In God I can't believe.
Nor do I logically perceive - -
No way can I see - no way can I hear
What many believe - to me it's not clear,
This God they talk about
That makes some preachers shout.
A God of good in this world of pain,
With so many diseased and on battlefields slain
I argue - it seems unreal to me,
How illogical, I say, can these believers be?"

The agnostic - he sits wonderingly on the religion fence
To believers the world over, he wishes no offence.
But if by aid of a slide rule, he could surely measure God;
Or view him through a telescope - through all tests of science plod
And God showed up by ultra scan or sophisticated X/Ray,
Allegiance to the Christian's God scientifically would prove OK

But God has given us special eyes to view His Majesty,
His spirit He will share with man in to eternity
In Eden, loved to walk beside the children he had made
He walked with Adam and his wife e'en through the verdant glade.
Before sin came, God's Love was real, the fountain of all life;
But all this changed when Adam fell, along with his wayward wife

For unbelief was born the day the voice of God was shunned
And from the face of man, that day, the face of God was turned
Man's Godly spirit withered, died, when sin spread o'er the earth
And all was lost, except a Saviour came by human birth.
From ancient times Jesus was planned to come and save our soul.
With promise that one day His grace will banish all things foul,

For Jesus suffered pain and grief upon that cross of shame;
But rose triumphant from the dead that we might do the same;
To save the world and put things right between mankind and God
His saving Love is free to all who rest upon his Word
To free us from the curse of death is why the Saviour came.
To prove to all the evil powers Jehovah's Glorious Name

When Jesus comes to cleanse the hearts of all who to Him fly.
His Spirit opens up again our spirit's inner eye;
The secret is to worship Him when cleansed from sin and shame
Yielding our heart - His Spirit will our fallen nature tame.
To seek His Face with gratitude and yearnings for His Grace
By meditating on His words, we'll surely glimpse His Face.
Then we can walk with God again,
As long ago, on Eden's plane.

There will be A New World -

We have yet to see the re-appearance of this Jesus of Nazareth, glorified and reigning as the Heavenly Powered King over a new trouble-free Kingdom on a completely new earth! This development will be a future fulfilment of dramatic prophecies.

His first Coming was a prophecy that was fulfilled. The prophecy that he is to come again as a triumphant King to rule over a kingdom of peace and justice will surely be fulfilled. Many people feel that it may happen in their life- time!

Geoff 'heard' these words as clear as a bell -

"My Son will rule in complete Truth: he will overwhelm the whole earth. In Majesty and Power He will reign - I in him and he in Me." Wow!!

Check with - ITim1: 17. Rev15: 3-4

The Lord keeps saying in various places –"**Time is short!"**

The Bible warns that there are to be terrible changes and destruction of the old flawed systems to pave the way for the New. We are seeing global changes now. They will get worse... much worse.

There may be no difficulty in looking forward to the fulfilment of future Bible prophesies as so many of them have already come to pass. There are many Bible studies to confirm this.

Free Access to Almighty God -

The amazing thing is that God does not require that we clean up our lives before we approach him, only that we are humbly willing for changes to take place in our personality and life through the leading and empowering of his Spirit -

This all-embracing God is the mystery of the good news (the Gospel) that is not known to many, which many have ignored or disbelieved.

It is never too late to make a fresh start, unless the heart has become hardened and insensitive; it is never too late to cry out to God for his mercy and help - Whatever our regrets, guilt, sins and past pains, there is always a vibrant hope if God is invited into the sadness or mess of our lives!

"The Lord ... is not willing that any should perish, but that all should come to repentance." King James - 2nd letter of Peter Chap3 verse9

HE IS LONGING TO ANSWER A PRAYER OF REPENTANCE,

- WHOEVER MAKES IT

God has promised to wipe away all tears one day in a gloriously new future. Mysteries will be revealed. So we must get up and look up to that higher world! It is waiting for us to step into! Then a New World *Within* will light up! Will fire up! And we shall know in our hearts that –

AT THE END OF THE DAY, ALL, ALL WILL BE WELL!
ALL THANKS AND PRAISE TO OUR
CREATOR FATHER GOD!

A Final Word From Geoff

I was given this wonderful Gift of Faith-and-Hope. The Gift is there on the proverbial 'table' for anyone who will, to reach out, to grasp and make their own!

APPENDIX

The beliefs and claims in the preceding chapters have their base on the following pronouncements of Jesus. The ones quoted are taken mainly from St John's Gospel in the New Testament of The Holy Bible, except where otherwise stated.

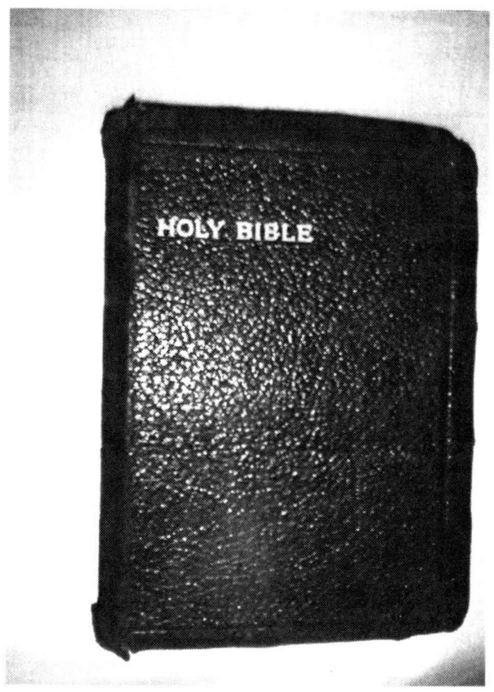

The all-encompassing claims of Jesus -
"I am the Way, the Truth and the Life."
Chapter 14 verse 6

Jesus made a sweeping statement- **"I am the resurrection and the Life, he who believes in me, though he die yet shall he live, and whoever lives and believes in me shall never die!"** Chapter 11 verse 23

The promise of eternal life is written in the following verses -

"If you continue in my word, you are truly my disciples, and you will know the truth, and the truth will make you free. ... Truly truly, I say to you, if anyone keeps my word he will never see death" Chapter 8 verses 31-32 &51

Specific attitudes of mind/heart are necessary to enable one to step up to the Higher Plane: -

Humility - that we are subject to, answerable to, and dependent on - a Higher Power,

Repentance - in awareness of an inclination to self-focus and self-interest with undesirable traits and flaws – this is 'sin'.

Submission - for changes to take place in all aspects and aims of our life. To let go the trivia and change priorities.

Faith - in Jesus Christ's rock-like promises and resulting obedience to his teaching.

Martha, sister of Mary and Lazarus made a tremendous discovery-

"I believe that you are the Christ, the Son of God, he who is coming into the world." Chapter 11 verse 27.

Jesus proves that he is The Life by raising the man Lazarus to life, stinking after being dead four days.

"Lazarus! Come out!" Chapter 11 verse 43.

Paul declared his assurance of a 'heavenly dwelling' – a new glorious body after physical death.

"For we know that if the earthly tent we live in is destroyed, we have a building from God, a house not made with hands, eternal in the heavens. Here indeed we groan and long to put on our heavenly dwelling" 2 Corinthians Chapter 5 verses 1 & 2

"For me to live is Christ, and to die is gain" He wrote to the Philippians in chapter 1 verse 21

The Peace formula that Jesus promised –

"Let not your hearts be troubled, you believe in God, believe also in me..."

Chapter 14 verse 1.

After some very difficult to understand teaching many stopped following Jesus; sadly he asked his intimate group, the twelve disciples,

"Will you also go away?"

Simon Peter whose spiritual eyes were opened answered him, **"Lord, to whom shall we go? Thou hast the words of eternal life; and we believe and are sure that thou art that Christ, the Son of the living God."** Chapter 6 verses 66 to 69.

(King James version.)

No one has a right, or basis, to argue against these people – these witnesses of the remarkable and miraculous events of that time.

Jesus makes it clear that he represents a Higher Power by saying in a loud voice of authority **"He who believes in me believes not in me but in him who sent me. And he who sees me sees him who sent me. I have come as light into the world that whoever believes in me may not remain in darkness."-** Chapter 12 verses 44 & 45.

The resurrected Jesus made this wonderful promise to his followers - "... **lo, I am with you always, even to the end of the world."** Matthew 28 verse 20 (King James version)

Jesus summarises God's Commandments **–"The first (commandment) is ... you shall love the Lord your God with all your heart, and with all your soul, and with all your mind and with all your strength.**

The second is this; you shall love your neighbour as yourself.

There is no other commandment greater than these." Mark 12 verses 29-31

NOTE

In no way am I a Historian so do not claim any scholarly knowledge about world history.
Nor have I studied Theology
Scriptural quotes are taken from the Revised Standard Version of the Holy Bible except where otherwise stated. D W

About The Author

Dorothy was born in a village in Bradford W Yorkshire. She was living in London when she met Geoffrey Ralph Wood. A quick engagement followed and in 1973, 10months later, aged 38yrs she married Geoff when he was aged 44yrs.

She qualified in Mental and General Nursing. After moving to S Wales and marrying Geoff she became a Social Worker and subsequently obtained the Certificate of Qualification in Social Work.

Interests have been: music- Beethoven to The Beatles, singing, mostly in church choirs - walking - reading - psychology - humour and gardening. She has written poems, letters and articles for books, local magazines, and press.

With a Methodist background, by a positive public step of faith aged fifteen years, Dorothy began to experience the reality of God for herself, and for the rest of her life.

For most of her life she has been involved in Christian Worship and Service; also taking interest in other faiths and a wide spectrum of religious experience, belief and thought.

Printed in the United Kingdom by
Lightning Source UK Ltd., Milton Keynes
139322UK00002B/37/P